WE'LL ALWAYS HAVE LISBON

HAVE LISBON

CELTIC'S GLORY YEAR 1967

WE'LL ALWAYS HAVE LISBON

CELTIC'S GLORY YEAR 1967

David Frier and Pat Woods

Photo Credits:-
Photograph 1 was originally published in *Stadión*, permission to reproduce this image has been sought. Photographs 2, 3, 4, 5, 8, 9, 10, 12, 13, 14, 19, 24, 26, 27, and 28 were originally published in *A Bola*, (c) ASF. Photographs 11, 16, 18, 22 and 23 and the photograph on the back cover were originally published in *O Século Ilustrado* and are reproduced courtesy of the *Hemeroteca* (Municipal Journal Archive) in Lisbon. Photographs 7, 15, 20, 21 and 25 were originally published in *Flama* and are reproduced courtesy of the *Hemeroteca* in Lisbon. The right to reproduce photograph 6 was kindly offered by Miguel de Paiva Couceiro, and it is (c) Miguel de Paiva Couceiro. Photograph 17 was originally published in *Europa Cup 1967-1968*, a special edition of the weekly paper *Revu*, permission to reproduce this image has been sought. Photographs 29 and 30 were supplied by *The Herald* and are (c) The *Herald* and *Times* Group. The photograph on the front cover of the book is a reproduction of a picture postcard of the National Stadium, Lisbon, shot during the first half of the European Cup final of 1967; there was no indication of a copyright holder on the original for this image.

ISBN 978-0-9957064-0-8

Design, Typesetting and origination by Peter Mason (www.pmasondesign.com)

Printed and bound in Great Britain by CMP (UK) Ltd.

CONTENTS

ACKNOWLEDGEMENTS (DAVID FRIER)

This has been a long and painstaking project over many years, and there are countless people who have given me assistance in a variety of respects: firstly, of course, Pat Woods, for all of his hard work and his extensive knowledge of all things related to Celtic, as well as Richard McBrearty and his staff at the Scottish Football Museum at Hampden. In Scotland, I should also mention members of my family and close friends who have offered me support and interest in this project at various times. And thanks are also due to Simon Hart for first putting me in touch with Pat.

In Portugal, I would wish to thank particularly the staff at the National Library; the National Archives; the Lisbon City Archives; the curators of the journals collection at the city's *Hemeroteca*, and in particular João Carlos Oliveira for his assistance in obtaining copies of the photographs held in their collections; to Carlos Marques and Nuno Rita at *A Bola* for their assistance in obtaining copies of the excellent photographs from that newspaper; to Alexandre Pereira, of the Portuguese Football Federation; to Captain Tiago Lourenço Lopes, the Curator of the Archive of the Portuguese Republican Guard, not least for successfully identifying the senior policeman who is photographed alongside Billy McNeill and the European Cup; and, finally, to Anne Stroobant at the National Sports Museum in Lisbon for her helpful assistance in my research on issues specifically relating to the National Stadium.

Elsewhere, I also received helpful assistance from the staff of the city *Hemeroteca* in Madrid; from the National Archives at Kew; from Rianne van de Wetering at the archives of Ajax Amsterdam (regarding the European Cup trophy); and from Jörg Jakob at *Kicker* magazine in Germany and Brendan Birch at the *Deutscher Fussballbund*, in enabling me to make contact with the match referee, Kurt Tschenscher. It was only shortly after I spoke to Herr Tschenscher about his memories of the Lisbon final that, sadly, he passed away in August 2014, and I am grateful to his daughter and son-in-law, Rolf and Brigitte Klein, for the further information which they sent me about him at what must have been a very difficult time for them.

I would also like to thank Miguel de Paiva Couceiro in Belgium for taking the time to conduct the extensive interview with me which forms the basis for chapter 8 of the book, as well as for copies of various press cuttings from the 1960s. Thanks are also due to Peter Mason for his painstaking work on processing the manuscript and creating the cover design.

Above all, I owe a huge debt of thanks to the patience and constant support of Rhian Atkin, who has humoured and encouraged my fascination with a football team of long ago and who has frequently offered her own excellent insights into Portugal in the 1960s, as well as offering practical advice throughout the project. I really couldn't have done it without her!

And finally, there is another group of people without whom this book would never have come into being: the Lisbon Lions themselves (including those squad players who did not take to the field in Lisbon but who played their part during that wonderful year), and to Jock Stein and his staff. You changed the world for many Scots on that day in Lisbon, and you helped one particular Bhoy to dream of a wider world...

ACKNOWLEDGEMENTS (PAT WOODS)

Pat Woods would like to thank the following: firstly, David Frier for his superb work. The staffs of the following institutions were extremely helpful: the Mitchell Library (Glasgow), the National Library of Scotland (Edinburgh), the British Library (London) and the *Bibliothèque Nationale* (Paris), a library which surely has the largest collection of newspapers from all parts of Europe. Laura McCallum did an excellent job of audiotyping on his behalf, while Jamie Fox, Ian McCallum and Bill Campbell were of great assistance in publishing and pre-production matters. Thanks are also due to the following for their help and encouragement: Sally Leslie (Pat's sister), Terry Dick, John McLauchlan, Archie Macpherson, Rodger Baillie, Hugh MacDonald, Gerry McNee, the McAlindon family (Lucy senior and junior, and Patricia), Frank Arrighi, Allan Herron, Gordon Cowan, David Potter, Tommy McGinn and Tommy Collin.

ABOUT THE AUTHORS

David Frier is formerly Senior Lecturer in Portuguese at the University of Leeds and is now an Honorary Research Fellow at the same institution. He has published widely on various aspects of Portuguese history and culture and is a lifelong Celtic supporter.

Pat Woods was born in Bangor, North Wales, in June 1946 but has lived in Glasgow for most of his life. He is the author/ co-author of ten other books on Celtic F.C. He has watched Celtic at home and abroad, including the 1967 European Cup final in Lisbon.

FOREWORD

Why yet another book about Celtic's victory in Lisbon in 1967? The main aspects of the story of Celtic's most successful season are surely well known to every supporter of the club: the remarkable transformation within two years from Scottish also-rans to champions of Europe; the thrilling defeat of the ultra-defensive Inter Milan of Helenio Herrera on a hot, sunny day in the Portuguese capital; the (perhaps understandably) over-enthusiastic celebrations of the Celtic supporters after the match; and the friendly support of the Portuguese for the Scottish underdogs in the *Estádio Nacional* on May 25th 1967.

However, both authors of this book have long felt that there must be other stories to tell: some previous books have included references to newspaper reports on the 1967 final from France, Spain and Italy, but strangely never (or very rarely) from the host country. The idea of a different type of book on Lisbon 1967, one which would tell the story of the final partly from the perspective of the Portuguese and, indeed, from a range of sources across Europe, first came to co-author David Frier during a period of study leave from Leeds University in Lisbon in March 2006. It was while he was having his hair cut in a small barbershop in the Estrada de Benfica that a hairdresser (recognising a slight foreign accent in his otherwise very good Portuguese) asked him where he was from: when he said from Scotland, the barber immediately asked "But Jimmy Johnstone? Did you hear that he has died?" And that was how he found out about the passing of one of his childhood heroes (reported in the Portuguese sports newspaper *A Bola* that very morning), and before long several older men (David included) in the barbershop were busy discussing **that** day at the National Stadium, when Jinky and ten others brought down the might of Inter Milan – and it was clear that all those taking part in this conversation had very fond (if now fading) memories of that team and that match.

So he realised that some day he would have to examine the Portuguese angle on this, the most important match in Celtic's history. Luckily, over the years Pat Woods had compiled an unrivalled range of reports, photographs and other materials relating to both May 1967 and the Jock Stein years at Celtic in general, and he too shared the desire to offer new perspectives on this historic match and also to get away from the temptation of painting everything in glowing colours: contemporary perspectives on this final (many of them recorded here) indicate just how tough a task Celtic faced throughout season 1966-67. The tendency today to view Celtic's victory in the final as an inevitability does not represent the reality at the time, and this book helps to chart the way in which Jock Stein's Celtic gradually chipped away at theapparent invincibility of their opponents before gaining their worthy reward.

And having conducted extensive research (often of material which has never before appeared in Scotland), yes, it is very pleasant to report that it does indeed seem that Celtic had the broad backing of the Portuguese public, both within the stadium and in Lisbon in general. This book offers some reasons why this may have been the case: notably historical tensions between Inter and Benfica, but also certain contemporary factors external to the sporting arena, while one chapter of this book will focus on an unfairly neglected Portuguese 'secret agent' who performed a valuable role in generating support for the Scots in Lisbon. Exploring these completely unexpected stories has been one of the greatest pleasures in working on this book. We also reveal how (and why) the final developed into a highly personal contest between the rival coaches, Jock Stein and Helenio Herrera; the story is also told, for the first time, of why the final came close to not being played in Portugal at all, and why the *Estádio Nacional*, unsuitable in many respects, was eventually chosen as the venue (and an enchanting one at that). We are confident that readers of this book will be interested to read these and other new insights into Celtic's victorious European campaign of 1967. So there are new stories to be told about Lisbon after all... and we hope that this book may stimulate the curiosity of others to look further into other Lisbon stories which have still to be told.

Finally, an explanation of the title of this book. *We'll Always have Lisbon* is a paraphrase of a famous line near the end of the 1942 movie *Casablanca*, where Rick Blaine (played by Humphrey Bogart) reminds Ilsa Lund (played by Ingrid Bergman) before she boards a flight from Casablanca to Lisbon (a 'neutral' transit point for refugees from World War II) that "We'll always have Paris", a reference to their pre-Occupation romance in the French capital. Not for nothing was Lisbon often dubbed 'Casablanca II' because of the similar ambience existing in the Portuguese capital during the Second World War.

David Frier and Pat Woods.

CHAPTER 1
"Let's not expect miracles..." *

Lisbon, May 25th 1967, around midnight or early morning of the 26th. The post-match celebrations were over, the wives and sweethearts had been sent to their plane at the airport and the players were making their way back to their hotel in Estoril, happy yet subdued as the excitement of winning the European Cup was wearing off, when John Rafferty of *The Scotsman* was witness to a Celtic supporter's outburst accompanied by a grin that was fixed by wine and pride: "Look at them – champions of Europe. Not so long ago they were a load of rubbish." The term was harsh, but it was not provocative, said Rafferty, for it was "the insulting exaggeration allowed amongst friends in Glasgow." It was the ultimate, if indirect, "affectionate regard", indeed tribute, to the incredible transformation that Jock Stein had wrought on an ailing club in the space of little more than two years.

The dizzy heights reached in the *Estádio Nacional* a few hours earlier could not possibly have been envisaged in the mid-winter of 1964-65 when the Glasgow club was heading for yet another season, the seventh in succession, without a major trophy to its name. The support, sullen and apathetic, was drifting away. Bluntly, the truth could no longer be ignored that, for all their wonderful tradition, Celtic had become just another club. However, regarding the announcement at a dramatic press conference on Sunday 31st January 1965, that Jock Stein, then manager of Hibernian, a man who had acquired a reputation as a physician for ailing clubs (and who was said to be a motivator and a transformer of fortunes without peer), would be taking over from the venerable Jimmy McGrory as Celtic manager as soon as the Edinburgh club acquired a new man at the helm, it should not be forgotten that this change would not have taken place but for an admission of failure on the part of the

---

*These words are an extract from the final sentence of Jock Stein's statement of intent in his first Celtic matchday programme of March 13th 1965. The remainder of the sentence reads "but may all of us in the non–distant future be sharing in great Celtic success".

club's autocratic chairman, Bob Kelly. Kelly recalled at this press conference that "the club was almost boycotted" in late 1951 when he brought Stein to the club as a player ("Jock Who?" and "Too old!" were the fans' reactions). Kelly was not the type to relinquish power (which, most contentiously of all, included interference in team selection), but his age and ailing health were taking their toll, as he explained in a 1969 interview with the journalist, Rodger Baillie: "I could still talk to the players in the 50s, the ones when Jock Stein played. But in the 60s, they looked on me as an old man. We needed someone who could talk their language, and we needed to make the change when we had a chance of success." That chance was taken in quick and dramatic fashion on Stein's forty-eighth day in charge of the club, with a Scottish Cup final victory over Dunfermline Athletic that was both the gateway to the greatest era in the club's history and further confirmation of the remarkable ability of the new man at the helm to quickly impose his personality on his players, to instil in them a belief that they were capable of beating anyone. Bobby Lennox recently recalled the revolution when Jock Stein took over in early March 1965: "Training, tactics, preparation - everything changed. We started training with the ball all the time. We still did a lot of running and worked hard, but we had the ball all the time."

Stein's plans required the inculcation of a greater degree of collective responsibility, as Billy McNeill revealed in an April 1967 *World Sports* interview when he stated that the new manager wanted him to be more assertive onfield: "I was given authority when I was made captain [in 1963], but I was reluctant to use it. I was brought up in football with these boys [the 'Kelly Kids'] and it was hard to bring authority to bear on them. Fortunately Celtic are now such a professional organisation that there is no awkwardness over orders." He would later expand on the pre-Stein era by observing that "It's sometimes forgotten that players like Bobby Murdoch and myself, and the others who grew up around the same time, had to forge our own traditions – we had known the heartbreak of defeat long before we learned the joy of climbing up first at cup presentations to collect the winners' medals." On European Cup final day itself, full back Tommy Gemmell was quoted in the *Scottish Daily Mail*'s preview as follows: "Looking back, I wonder what would have happened if we hadn't the good luck to get Mr. Stein as boss of Celtic. It had always been a happy club. But something almost inexplicable occurred within two days of him being installed as team manager [a reference to a 6-0 victory at Airdrie]. For myself, I got a new lease of life. Instead of playing football off the cuff, we got method. Team spirit improved. We acquired a certain amount of class. Gone was apprehension. The team style was radically altered. Instead of being just a full back, playing routine, orthodox pattern, I became an attacking full back in a 4-2-4 set-up. The game began to get exciting. We were really alive. There were indications that one day we would be a side to be feared in Europe."

Consistency was the central theme Stein preached from the outset of his management, hammering home the message that one-off triumphs such as the Scottish Cup final victory were not good enough for a club with the traditions of Celtic. That demand was to be tested to the limit in his first full season at Parkhead. In its first edition (of August 1965) the Scottish monthly magazine *Goal* conveyed a sense of relish – shared by supporters of both clubs – in its anticipation of the battle for power between Celtic and Rangers by using the headline "No Surrender!" (bearing connotations unique to football in Glasgow) above an article which predicted that Rangers would shrug off the challenge of the "new Celtic" and "steam-roller their way through the new season", while elsewhere in the magazine there was a side-swipe at "the hysterical heights of near idolatry" to which Jock Stein had been raised by press and public alike, described as "the blind believers in Stein as a supernatural being." The latter was under pressure from the start of season 1965-66, even admitting at the end of it that his chairman, Bob Kelly, had made it clear to him that he would be a "very disappointed man" if the club did not win the championship for the first time in twelve years. Understandably, the manager gave short shrift to a supporter who in the close season had asked him if Celtic were getting the flagpole ready for the League Championship flag. In the very first edition of the club magazine *Celtic View* (August 11th 1965), he outlined the challenge in stark terms: "None of us must assume that because Celtic have had some recent success everything good will follow. We are not a great team, but we are a team of great promise. There will be no let-up in our efforts, however, to become a great team. We must go all out to make Celtic again one of the great names in world football."

The manager had already taken a significant step to restoring Celtic's prestige by signing Joe McBride, a prolific goalscorer, from Motherwell for a bargain fee of £22,500 in June 1965. In his first season at his new club he would amass 43 goals in 51 matches in all competitions, both domestic and European. His prowess in front of goal helped to bring Celtic an early dividend with the club's first League Cup triumph since 1957, a bruising 2-1 victory (thanks to penalty awards converted by John Hughes) in the October 1965 final over a Rangers side which had already served notice that it would not be found wanting in its determination to retain its longstanding post-war domination over its oldest rivals and which had the distinct advantage of having in their squad the likes of Ritchie, Greig, McKinnon, Henderson, Forrest, Millar and Wilson, all of whom had title-winning experience. The Ibrox club had amassed thirty-four league titles to Celtic's twenty before Stein took over the reins at Celtic and were confident that they could extend that massive lead with the blend of strength and direct football that had characterised their most successful teams.

Unencumbered by European participation, Rangers went undefeated in the League Championship until Christmas Day 1965, when Dunfermline Athletic's first ever victory at Ibrox Park (3-2) allowed Celtic to top the table on goal average with an 8-1 home victory over Morton (7-0 at half-time!) which included a McBride hat-trick. Celtic's 5-1 rout of Rangers on an icy home pitch on January 3rd 1966 was marked by Steve Chalmers' hat-trick in addition to sending them two points clear at the top, but those fans in green and white who wrote off Rangers as potential champions were all too soon disabused of that notion by three successive away defeats for Celtic (at Aberdeen, Heart of Midlothian and Stirling Albion), which put paid to any notions of a procession to the title and restored Rangers as league leaders as the month of February 1966 drew to a close. It would take 'Black March', when Rangers lost twice and drew twice, to undermine the Light Blues' surge and make Celtic odds-on for the title.

By the middle of the following month, after the European Cup-Winners' Cup semi-final first leg 1-0 home victory over Liverpool on April 14th 1966 before an all-ticket crowd numbering 80,000, Celtic were in a position to achieve a clean sweep of all the honours available to them. The League Cup was already in the bag: they were favourites to beat Rangers in the Scottish Cup Final which was due to be played on April 23rd and follow that up by clinching the League title; and the season might end with a European Cup-Winners' Cup final scheduled for Hampden Park. However, that rosy prospect disintegrated as the result of a sudden, alarming failure to find the net. Astonishingly, Celtic fired only blanks for 445 minutes, the virtual equivalent of five matches, following Bobby Lennox's 50th-minute goal against Liverpool at Parkhead. Two days later Celtic drew a league match with Hibernian (0-0) at Easter Road, then lost 0-2 three days afterwards at Liverpool in the return Cup-Winners' Cup tie (an aggregate 1-2 exit), although a late (and wrongly disallowed) Lennox goal would have taken Celtic to the final on the away goals rule. Disappointment turned to sheer misery when they lost the Scottish Cup final replay (0-1) to Rangers on April 27th after a goalless first match. Two trophies had been put out of reach in the space of nine days, and now only the League title was left to play for. Make no mistake, Celtic fans were now deeply concerned by their favourites' goal famine and by the prospect of a resurgent Rangers taking advantage of Celtic's goal drought and fighting their way back into title contention after snatching the Scottish Cup against the odds.

Had Celtic's momentum stalled fatally at a crucial time? With the finishing post in sight, Celtic's next league match was at Greenock on April 30th against a Morton side which needed victory to avoid relegation. The position at the top before kick-off was as follows (in a 34-match schedule, with the title being decided by goal average in the event of a points tie) :-

Celtic - played 31, 51 points, 101 goals for, 29 against.

Rangers - played 32, 51 points, 85 goals for, 28 against.

Jock Stein's greatest fear, kept under wraps until the season had ended, was that their greatest rivals, a challenger replete with championship medals that testified to their "knowing how to pace themselves for the final effort", would ultimately prevail. In his matchday preview in the *Glasgow Herald*, Raymond Jacobs said that Celtic faced a stern examination of their resolution and resources as they neared the climax of their "long and grinding struggle for a league championship which not so long ago seemed comfortably within their reach." Looking back shortly afterwards at that fraught encounter at a packed Cappielow, Celtic captain Billy McNeill recalled a heart-stopping moment in the 30th minute when, with the teams locked at 0-0, the home side was awarded a penalty after Jimmy Johnstone, back helping out in defence, upended Morton striker Alan McGraw: "If they score from this, we are in trouble", thought McNeill. That sounds like an understatement when one considers that a hush descended on the ground as an "ashen-faced" Johnstone and an anxious Celtic support looked on as a penalty kick was about to be taken which could have grim, potentially fatal consequences for Celtic's title hopes, not to mention the concomitant opportunity for Celtic to take part in the European Cup for the first time. Harry Andrew of the *Scottish Sunday Express*, who had been witnessing a Celtic minus the injured Joe McBride and John Hughes and clearly out of touch, suffering, he believed, from the effects of the Liverpool and Rangers defeats and showing no semblance of the form which had brought them so much glory that season, captured the moment in stark terms: "This was the moment on which perhaps everything hung... the title, relegation and all the things that go with them."

Allan Herron of the *Sunday Mail* described what happened next: "Up came Flemming Nielsen, the Dane with no.10 on his back, who had been showing a thirst for battle in the early stages. But oh, what a mess he made of it! Calmly, he placed the ball, didn't bother to line himself up properly, then turned and cleared the crossbar by at least four feet... Disaster, I felt, for Morton. A blood transfusion for Celtic." Jack Harkness of the rival *Sunday Post* noted "the pandemonium in the Celtic ranks as the Dane lashed the ball high over the bar", while Billy McNeill remembered that "I don't know who breathed their sigh of relief more loudly – us, or our supporters." The let-off acted as a spur to Celtic, more particularly Jimmy Johnstone, who in the last minute of the first half ran diagonally into the box to latch on to an astute Bertie Auld pass and hammer the ball into the far corner of the net, albeit with the aid of a deflection, just as the referee was set to blow for half time.

Shortly after the interval, the normally reliable McGraw passed up a golden opportunity for a Morton equaliser when, unmarked at the back post, he failed to make a proper connection with Wilson's low cross, the ball rolling off his shin a yard or so from the goal-line before being scrambled clear. "What confidence a goal hereabouts would have given Morton – and how it might have shaken Celts", said Jack Harkness. Thereafter, Celtic took a firm grip on the contest and went on to clinch victory in the dying seconds, Johnstone redeeming himself for the second time that afternoon, this time with a cross that enabled Bobby Lennox to outjump keeper Sørensen and make it 2-0. Celtic held their nerve in the remaining two matches, coming from behind to defeat Dunfermline Athletic 2-1 at home before sealing the championship with a 1-0 victory at Motherwell, Lennox's last-minute goal meeting the manager's demand that Celtic annex the championship by a two-point margin rather than settling for the draw or the narrow defeat which would guarantee the title on goal average, a testimony to how close that ninety minutes in Greenock had come to derailing the most glorious period in the club's history, particularly since Rangers had not faltered in the closing stages, winning their final seven league matches.

Stein was big enough to admit to Allan Herron in the *Sunday Mail* of May 8th 1966 that he had made mistakes during the season, though he did not elaborate on this statement, merely adding "who is to say whether it would have changed anything?" Whatever, he had succeeded in extracting every ounce of effort and commitment from a squad which had no previous acquaintance with the winning feeling. Many of his players, said Stein, "gave me more than I expected", an indication of how much of a learning process the season had been for both the players and the man who had guided them to glory. Jimmy Johnstone, a rather wayward figure before the new manager began to impose his authority on the club, gave an insight into the regime change in an interview with the *Sunday Post* (March 20th 1966), in which he revealed that previously he believed that he had played a great game if he had simply beaten plenty of opponents: "We always had the will to win, but what we have now is the knowledge of how to win. We know exactly how we are going to play before we go out. Mr. Stein has made me realise that the man off the ball can often contribute more than the player on it."

Similarly, in an interview of March 6th 2010 with Hugh MacDonald of *The Herald,* Billy McNeill endorsed Johnstone's observation that the off-the-cuff approach was now history. The captain said that "he would have been off" [apparently to Tottenham Hotspur. with a fourfold wage hike] had Jock Stein not returned to Celtic Park as manager, then outlined the importance of a growing bond to the early successes of his reign: "Big Jock taught us to respect each other in the team. He also taught us to respect the people who supported us. We were hard guys in the proper sense. None of us appreciated fools. We recognized each other's abilities. We fought and argued with each other like nobody's business. We argued over nothing, we argued over everything. But we had an attitude. It was this: if we could give of our best, then opponents would have great difficulty in beating us." He added that there were "verbal and physical battles among the players (not too often), but we set a standard and if someone was not meeting it, then, well …"

Jock Stein encouraged that attitude, believing that it instilled a serious competitive edge, and the five-week tour of Bermuda, the United States of America and Canada which followed hard upon the title win just reinforced the growing perception that a period of endless possibilities awaited the Scottish champions. Part holiday, part testing ground where moves and tactics were experimented with and rough edges smoothed, it provided the squad with a platform to showcase their burgeoning skills and develop that intensely competitive mindset and edge which hastened their development into a formidable force: "Nobody could be shy and retiring", said the Celtic captain, "Nobody could take a step back." While the players were demonstrating the enhanced level of professionalism demanded by Stein by fulfilling their determination to end the eleven-match schedule unbeaten (including matches against Tottenham Hotspur and Bayern Munich), the likes of Bobby Lennox was enabled to hone his blistering pace and finishing power, Joe McBride to underline his deadly marksmanship, and Bertie Auld and Bobby Murdoch given further scope to perfect their midfield partnership. More significantly, perhaps, Jock Stein used the tour as a means of getting to know his squad in greater depth and, just as important, giving his players the opportunity to get better acquainted with each other.

And it worked a treat, causing Jock Stein, wearing a trilby hat at a jaunty angle, to emerge with a broad grin from the plane at Glasgow Airport on the party's arrival back in Scotland, positively glowing with satisfaction and a sense of expectancy about the season to come. His demeanour was wholly in keeping with a man who in his recent press musings had given the impression that he would never feel totally fulfilled in his profession until he won the trophy that had become the Holy Grail of European club football.

CHAPTER 2
The Magnificent Obsession

Springtime in Paris has its undeniable attractions, such as shopping, dining at a prestigious restaurant, and attending the cabaret/burlesque show at the famous Lido on the Champs Elysées. Such were the pleasures enjoyed by the delegates of selected clubs invited by the sports daily *L'Equipe* to attend a meeting in the Hotel Ambassador on the Boulevard Haussmann on the morning of April 2nd 1955. The newspaper's initiative, the latest manifestation of the French genius for promoting sporting competition such as the Olympic Games (revived by Baron de Coubertin) and the World Cup (thanks to the vision of Jules Rimet), was a bold one, designed to find Europe's number one side in a competition which would involve the top clubs in Europe.

In 1903 the newspaper *L'Auto*, a by-product of the vicious partisanship surrounding the 'Dreyfus Affair' which had convulsed France around the turn of the century, had inaugurated an international cycle race, the famous Tour de France, in order to boost circulation, a ploy which bears an uncanny resemblance to the *raison d'être* of the European Cup. During the febrile atmosphere surrounding the liberation of Paris in August 1944, *L'Auto* was closed down for its perceived "submission to German control". The editor-in-chief of that newspaper, Jacques Goddet, a man compromised by his championing of Maréchal Pétain, the leader of the Vichy regime, nevertheless managed to launch in early 1946 a successor magazine, *L'Equipe* ('The Team'), its title apparently chosen to reflect the ideals of "pulling together" and solidarity that Goddet now called for to help repair a broken France, and, by extension, to distance the new journal from lingering suspicions about his own ambiguous past. *L'Equipe*'s take-up of *L'Auto*'s organisation of the Tour de France gave the fertile minds of a group of trailblazing sportswriters at *L'Equipe* - Gabriel Hanot, Jacques de Ryswick and Jacques Ferran - an invaluable insight into, and inspiration for, the promotion of sporting competitions. In the May 2016 edition of *UEFA Direct* the last surviving member of the founding fathers of the European Cup, 96-year-old Jacques Ferran, was at pains to underline just how much of a gamble the launching of the European Cup was and how much its introduction was due to the enterprise of the aforementioned journalists: "It wasn't the owner, the director or the boss. No, it was journalists who created the European Cup and the European Footballer of the Year award. We needed to get the boss's approval if we wanted to invent a competition, but when we went to see Jacques Goddet he welcomed us with open arms, because he thought primarily in economic terms. *L'Equipe* was a sports daily and we sold very few copies during the week – there was no football to write about on Tuesdays, Wednesdays or Thursdays. We rehashed old news, looking back on what had happened the previous Sunday and announcing as early as possible what was coming up on the following Sunday. But there was no reporting, no news. There wasn't enough to write about, so the creation of a European Cup to be contested during the week was a godsend."

However, everyone present at that fateful meeting was all too aware that the backing of the sport's governing bodies FIFA and UEFA (hitherto lukewarm about the idea) was essential to get the proposal off the ground, and this was where an element of poker, some might say blackmail, came in. The representatives of the hugely ambitious Real Madrid, Santiago Bernabeu (President of the club and a driving force without compare) and his right-hand man, Raimundo Saporta, pushed for the rules of such a competition – already drafted by Jacques Ferran - to be adopted immediately and unreservedly by those present and an organizational committee elected before submitting a proposal to FIFA. Ferran would recall that it was clear to everyone present that the tournament was going ahead, with or without the approval of FIFA or UEFA. The ploy, with its heavy connotations of being an idea whose time had come and which gave the impression of being a *fait accompli*, had been perfectly timed. One month later at an emergency FIFA meeting in London, the international body gave its approval to the competition on condition that it was endorsed by the national associations concerned and be organised under the auspices of the fledgling UEFA, which duly took charge of what it named the *Coupe des Clubs Champions Européens*, the European Cup.

A competition had been launched which had been in gestation for half a century, after the game took root on mainland Europe as a result of missionary work by clubs from Britain, which regarded itself as the home of football, to spread the gospel of football and foster its development. Celtic FC had made a notable contribution in that respect during the early decades of the twentieth century, starting with matches against enthusiastic beginners in Vienna and Prague in 1904, followed by visits to Denmark, Central Europe, France and

Switzerland prior to the Great War, and then being hailed afterwards as the "first swallows of peace" in the German press by defying officialdom in 1922 to become the first British club to play in that country since the cessation of hostilities: "it is our bounden duty to be friends with foemen and shake hands and resume life in the old way", said Celtic secretary-manager Willie Maley. During that latter tour of Central Europe the club again came into contact with a former player, Johnny Madden, who had been a member of Celtic's first ever eleven before eventually spending a quarter of a century as the coach/ trainer at Slavia Prague and who is credited with laying the foundations of the game in Czechoslovakia, a testimony to which was both his club's victory (3-2) over a Celtic side billed beforehand in the city as the "World's best team" and by the fact that 45 years later, when the Glasgow club returned to Prague on European Cup business, locals visited their hotel eager to remind captain Billy McNeill of the impact that Madden had made on the development of the game in their country.

Celtic's two defeats in Prague on that tour (the other was by Sparta) only underlined the growing perception that the pupils would soon become the masters, for all the lingering notions of British supremacy in world football. In central Europe, in particular, the rising standards would bring about the Mitropa Cup ('Mitropa' being an abbreviation of *Mitteleuropa* or Central Europe), inaugurated in 1927 for the top clubs in Austria, Hungary, Czechoslovakia, Yugoslavia and Italy. Initially highly popular, it lost its importance with the advent of war in 1939 and gradually declined post war, until at the time of its demise in 1992 the cup was being contested by second-division clubs. During its heyday, Johnny Madden was reputed, while in semi-retirement, to have been indirectly responsible for Slavia's victory over Ferencváros of Hungary in the 1938 final. Like the Latin Cup, inaugurated in 1949 for the top clubs of France, Portugal, Spain and Italy, the Mitropa Cup was a prototype for the first pan-European trophy, the European Cup. It is largely overlooked that the aforementioned four countries dominated the European Cup before Celtic's 1967 triumph, largely as a result of the invaluable experience that their clubs gained from the Latin Cup, a competition which also gave impetus to the aspirations of such as Gabriel Hanot, the most influential editorial presence in *L'Equipe* and its sister magazine, *France Football*. Simon Zimny, a defender in the Reims side which beat AC Milan in the 1953 Latin Cup final in Lisbon, recalled hearing in their *Estádio Nacional* dressing room his coach Albert Batteux discussing passionately with Hanot the prospects for, and the absolute necessity of, a genuine Europe-wide competition, including Britain (*France Football*, July 20th 2004), a testimony to the groundswell, on the Continent at least, for the game to reflect a more global, more co-operative post-war world.

Hanot's opportunity to turn a dream into reality came in December 1954 after watching Wolverhampton Wanderers' 'revenge' victory at Molineux over the Hungarian side, Honved, which included members of the national team which had inflicted two recent, heavy and humiliating defeats upon England (6-3 at Wembley, 7-1 in Budapest). The Midlands club's victory on a gluepot of a pitch which favoured the home side's more direct and forceful style, led to them being hailed in the English press as champions of the world, a designation which incensed Hanot, who insisted that Wolverhampton Wanderers would have to prove their invincibility by going to the likes of Budapest and Moscow (the latter being a reference to Wolves' earlier victory over Spartak), Madrid and Milan. Within six months of his advocacy Hanot saw his idea come to fruition. Jacques de Ryswick, one of the cadre of writers on *L'Equipe* enthused by the project, would state in his 1962 autobiography that but for the newspaper's determination the competition might never have seen the light of day. In truth, the internationally-minded Hanot had been aided by his capturing of the spirit of the times, his initiative coming only a decade after Europe had been plunged for a second time that century into a devastating conflict. In the early 1950s the European Coal and Steel Community had become the first concrete symbol of post-war co-operation, bringing together Belgium, Italy, France, West Germany, the Netherlands and Luxembourg in an organisation which was the nucleus of what became in 1957 the Common Market (now the European Union) from which initially Britain stood apart. UEFA itself had come into being in 1954; in lighter vein was the inaugural Eurovision Song Contest held in Switzerland in 1956.

However, nothing of a unifying nature, in terms of popularity and impact, would come to compare with the European Cup which – largely thanks to the dazzling Real Madrid (Di Stéfano, Puskas, *et al*) and the spread of television – captured the popular imagination. Billy McNeill, in his *Evening Citizen* (Glasgow) column published two days after Celtic's 1967 triumph, would recall how captivated he and his friends, fresh from taking part in a schoolboys' match, had been by the spectacle of watching in a café the TV coverage of Real Madrid edging out Reims in a thrilling 1956 final (the first) in Paris.

The competition was well on its way to becoming what one writer, Rob Hughes, has described as "The Cup of Dreamers and Magicians, the event to play in", but intriguingly its first decade saw challenges, albeit all abortive, to its format and organisation such as to make one wonder what the structure of the competition could have become by the time Celtic would have their first shot at becoming Europe's finest. A common theme to these proposed changes was the replacement of the European Cup by a European League which would guarantee the participating clubs a number of matches instead of involving the risk of an early knock-out, with its attendant impact on revenue. As early as May 1959, 'Waverley' (W. G. Gallacher) of the *Daily Record*, who was in Scandinavia to cover a Rangers tour and a Scottish vs. Jutland select match, was briefed by Danish football officials who had the ear of their countryman, UEFA president Ebbe Schwartz, on a proposal to introduce a "glamour league" whereby a "certain number of points matches" would enlarge the number of huge crowds. "Imagine, for instance", said 'Waverley', "the Ibrox terraces with successive visits from Real Madrid, Moscow Dynamo, Turin [Juventus] or Milano [A.C. Milan)], Reims, Barcelona and other glamourised combines from across the Channel." In April 1962, John F Wilson, chairman of Rangers, the most experienced British club in the competition to that date, and one greatly desirous of winning the trophy, was invited to a Paris meeting of "glamour clubs", among them Real Madrid, Barcelona and Arsenal, to discuss a proposal for a new "European Super League", as Jack Ronnie of the *Scottish Sunday Express* described it, and which would feature sixteen clubs to be split into groups of four, giving each participant at least six matches as they vied for the top place in each group, which would lead eventually to the winner of the competition being decided on a knock-out basis. Three years later, the caravan moved on to Amsterdam, where a French delegate to a UEFA meeting proposed that top clubs should form themselves into a 'European League' – two clubs from each selected country in a sixteen-club competition. Jack Harkness, in his *Sunday Post* report of October 24th 1965, noted that the clubs concerned would have to withdraw from their domestic leagues. If it came to pass, he envisioned a European league which included Celtic and Rangers from Scotland, Manchester United and Tottenham Hotspur from England, Real Madrid and Barcelona from Spain, Inter and AC Milan from Italy, Monaco and Saint-Etienne from France, Cologne and Eintracht Frankfurt from West Germany, Anderlecht and Standard Liege from Belgium, plus Austria FC and Rapid Vienna from Austria.

All three schemes foundered on the rocks of domestic considerations. National associations would not countenance the leading clubs being withdrawn from their competitions, thus depriving the other clubs of lucrative fixtures; seasons did not dovetail (consider, for example, winter shutdowns in Scandinavia and central Europe, while, especially in Britain, midweek European league fixtures would be impractical for arranging cup replays and postponed fixtures). However, one can clearly detect in these proposals the template for the Champions League which displaced the European Cup in 1992, but the former was but a twinkle in the eye of administrators as season 1966-67 loomed for Celtic FC. In front of them was a debut season in the European Cup, a tournament in which six of the previous participant clubs from the British Isles (including Ireland) who had reached the semi-finals had found that stage an impassable barrier in the first eleven seasons of the competition. The challenge of rewriting football history was given an additional edge by the fact that, remarkably (some might say embarrassingly) for a club with its standing and traditions, Celtic FC had been preceded by five other Scottish clubs in taking part in the most demanding of all football arenas.

The 1966-67 season was to be a 'first' in a number of ways other than Celtic's participation in the competition. The Lisbon final was to be one of many firsts: this was the first club match of such international stature to be played in Portugal (although, as noted above, a final of the Latin Cup, one of the predecessors of the European Cup, had also been played at the National Stadium in Lisbon); it was the first final to feature a British team; it was the first final won by a northern European team; it was the first final not to feature a team from the Iberian Peninsula; and it was also the first time that the participating teams would compete for a new trophy. The decision to adopt the latter could be said to have marked the point where UEFA definitively took control over the competition, and (as it turned out) it thus proved appropriate that this new trophy was introduced in the year when the competition finally ceased to be the exclusive preserve of teams from the south of Europe.

These facts relating to that trophy are not widely recognised today: after the 2014 Final in Lisbon, one TV commentator referred to Real Madrid "lifting this huge trophy for the tenth time." Yet in reality it was only for the fourth time: photographs of the club's earlier victories (most famously, at Hampden Park in 1960) show a much smaller trophy, the original one. Equally, in 1967 the iconic images - now so cherished by Celtic fans - of Billy McNeill posing with the Cup would have been all the more striking at the time precisely for the fact that the existence of a new trophy had barely been publicized, perhaps because UEFA was not as well resourced and equipped in that respect as it is today. The German football magazine *Kicker* highlighted the confusion, with a photograph of the original (1956-1966) trophy appearing on the front cover of its May 22nd 1967 edition and a photograph of the new one in a preview of the final on its inside pages, suggestive perhaps of a belated receipt of a photo of the new Cup affecting the production process, which may also explain why, on the morning of the match, Scottish newspapers were still using photographs of the original to accompany their previews. The official match programme adapted an image of the old trophy for its front cover design and, in pardonable ignorance, many Celtic fans in Lisbon purchased replicas of the original trophy which were on sale in the city centre. The latter, donated by *L'Equipe* to mark its inaugural role, had been modelled on the classical Greek amphora, a jar-shaped commemorative vase with two handles and a narrow neck that was awarded to victors in ancient sporting contests. It was certainly a handsome trophy, but it does not possess the magisterial air of the one to which we have become accustomed today. The replacement of the original trophy was partly a reflection of the growing recognition of the importance of the tournament during its early years, and, rather surprisingly, it did not have the names of the first eleven champions (1956-1966 inclusive) engraved on it. As we have seen, the initial years of the competition were approached cautiously by many (famously, the Football League prohibited Chelsea from taking part in its first season). As time went on, however, and the reach of television grew, so the glamour represented by clubs such as Real Madrid, Benfica and the two Milan sides, and by players such as Di Stéfano, Puskas, Eusébio and Mazzola raised the profile of the tournament amongst a mass audience across the continent and beyond: the Lisbon final was also covered by journalists and broadcasters from Argentina and Brazil, for example. By the mid-1960s, then, the European Cup had become a real object of desire.

The winners of the original trophy were permitted to make a full-size replica of it for display in their own trophy room (and, indeed, six identical trophies are on public display today at the Bernabeu Stadium in Madrid). However, by the time that Real Madrid had won the trophy for the sixth time (in Brussels in 1966), it appears that nobody was quite sure which of the trophies in their possession was the original one and which the imitations, and UEFA (now fully convinced of the value of the competition, not least with clubs like Inter being prepared to spend huge sums of money to ensure winning it) wished to share in the prestige and have its own logo engraved on the plinth of a trophy rather than the name of a journal (in the form 'Offert par *L'Equipe*') which had embarrassed them into promoting continental competition in a serious fashion. Naturally, the people at *L'Equipe* were miffed by what they saw as a slight, if not an act of base ingratitude, when the opportunity arose to make the change. In the autumn of 1966, following their sixth triumph, Real Madrid, always anxious to project their own image as the dominant club in Europe, requested the right to keep the initial trophy in perpetuity. This request was granted at a UEFA Executive meeting in Geneva in December 1966 (as reported in *A Bola*, of December 15th 1966).

The Cup won by Celtic in 1967 is now in the possession of Ajax (who were allowed to retain it after their three successive triumphs in the 1970s), and a photograph of the base of that trophy clearly displays the insignia of the Stadelmann family of jewellers and goldsmiths in Berne. The choice of Stadelmann to design and make the new trophy afforded UEFA secretary Hans Bangerter, based in the same Swiss city, the ideal opportunity to keep a close eye on the progress of the project. Jürg Stadelmann takes up the story in a 2006 UEFA brochure commemorating the fiftieth anniversary of the competition:

"My father Hans and I went along to Herr Bangerter's office and covered the whole floor with the drawings. He made comments like 'the Bulgarians would like the bottom of that, the Spaniards would like that, but the Italians would prefer that and the Germans would go for this bit...' We put the design together like a jigsaw puzzle. It was a 'bastardised' design, yet I like it and I think everyone in football likes it as well. I remember that it *had* to be finished by March 28th because I was getting married and taking my wife for a 10-day boat trip to Los Angeles. The trophy took 340 hours to make. I did the finer work, and then it was finished off by the engraver, Fred Banninger. On time, I am glad to say." A touch of intrigue was added to the story in the May /June 2015 edition of the German football magazine *Elf Freunde*, where a Horst Heeren claimed to have had a hand in the design in 1967.

The new trophy was 62 centimetres (approximately 2.5 feet) tall and weighed 7.5 kilograms (approximately 16 lbs.), with a gold-plated interior. In an article published in the *Berner Zeitung* in October 2012, Nicole Stadelmann, now the owner of the family firm, explained that the company was a natural choice for making the new trophy since it had frequently been commissioned to engrave winners' names on UEFA trophies in the past. The desire on UEFA's part to have a more impressive trophy is demonstrated by the specifications which were given to her father's company: it was to have two handles (their design accentuated to give the new trophy a distinctive identity and thus highlight its dramatic impact), enough capacity for three or four bottles of celebratory champagne, and a stately appearance which would make it easily recognisable. In addition, however, in order to obtain the prestigious contract, the company had to cede the intellectual property rights to the design to UEFA, so that when the trophy was last replaced (after Liverpool's triumph in 2005), Stadelmann were invited to tender for the replacement, but were unsuccessful in their bid. (The current trophy, produced by Koch und Bergfeld, in Bremen, is essentially identical to the one presented to Celtic, with the only readily identifiable difference being that the lettering on the front of the cup is now entirely in capital letters, whereas the previous versions of the trophy used a mixture of upper- and lower-case lettering.)

"It may not have been an artistic masterpiece", said Jürg Stadelmann," but everybody has been keen to get their hands on it". The contract loss may have broken a link with Celtic's greatest moment, you might say, but has there ever been a greater advert for the Cup than the sight of Billy McNeill thrusting it towards the skies?

CHAPTER 3
Bicycling to the Moon†

Celtic's *annus mirabilis* would be bookended by two great adventures, the aforementioned summer tour of 1966 and the European Cup final in May 1967. It could be said that Celtic's journey to the glory of Lisbon really began on the morning of May 11th 1966 (four days after the League title was clinched), when the squad gathered at Glasgow Airport at 8:45 a.m en route to Bermuda for an eleven-match tour spanning that island and the North American continent. There is ample testimony for the strengthening of Celtic's self-belief and team spirit generated by their journey across the North American continent, as instanced by an interview that Billy McNeill did with the sportswriter Hugh McIlvanney three decades later: "We did not all love one another but we developed the closeness of a big family… we were the usual cross section of personalities and temperament you expect in a group of football players but that tour impressed on us how much we depended on one another and how much more effective we would be if loyalty and trust were real." He added that Jock Stein could be easygoing when he thought it was appropriate and on that tour "was pretty lenient when he knew we weren't holding back on enjoying ourselves." We believed that Stein was "probably standing back and taking a good look at all of us, assessing us for the future – I believe, in the main, he saw what he hoped to see."

The sense of anticipation of a new season had undeniably been heightened when fans read transatlantic reports of the squad beginning to cloak itself in a sense of invincibility in what turned out to be a journey of self-discovery. The manager, although he would have been loath to speak about it, prepared

---

† The title for this chapter is taken from a statement by Real Madrid president Santiago Bernabeu in the mid-1960s that the challenge involved in winning the European Cup was "like riding a bicycle to the moon".

for the European Cup from the moment his players reported for pre-season training. Billy McNeill has often recalled the seriousness of purpose that was now becoming the hallmark of Celtic's approach to the game, an all-consuming work ethic which the captain regarded as the most significant component of the Celtic players' determination to maintain the standards they were now setting for themselves at the prompting of an ex-miner who was a product of the Lanarkshire coalfields, where he experienced the gruelling, dangerous work which imbued in men the values of teamwork ,a lesson he drummed into his players, who had earned the nickname 'Stein's stunners'.

Shortly after the Lisbon triumph, McNeill spoke of how (and where) the club's all-conquering season was forged and left no one in any doubt as to the identity of the man to whom most of the credit was due for Celtic going on to reach once inconceivable heights: "The more I look back to the European Cup triumph, I am convinced that far and away the principal reason for our success was the fact that even after a long, hard season, in which we had won all the home honours possible – the Glasgow Cup, the League Cup, the Scottish Cup and the League Championship – we did not reach the very peak of our form until we played in Lisbon. And for that one man must take most of the credit – our manager, Mr. Jock Stein. All through the season he had coached and coaxed us, he had gradually built a first team pool of players who had confidence in one another and in him. He had done more. The other players just as much as myself believed before 'Boss' Stein returned as manager to the club he once captained that we were Celts to the core. But the 'Boss' hammered into us day after day, week by week, as we progressed that we never could be sufficiently proud of playing for Celtic. He encouraged us to take every match as it came and not to lose sight of the weekly fixture through thinking too much of more important things to come. But as we went from success to success he subtly began to get us thinking there was more than just a possibility of winning the European Cup. We rehearsed move after move – chiefly in attack – in the peace and privacy of our training ground, Barrowfield Park. We talked and talked, we discussed and discussed. Everyone was encouraged to get into the picture; no idea was discarded until it had been proved ineffectual for Celtic's purposes. No club has done more preparing and planning, no club has worked harder than Celtic." It cannot be emphasised often enough how much the club's new-found reputation for fast, free-flowing and entertaining football with a winning dimension was underpinned by the values of hard work and application. Joe McBride said that the presence of fans looking on gave "an added edge, a special atmosphere" to those Celtic workouts.

Season 1966-67 had not yet officially begun when Celtic fans were given a firm indication that something special was taking shape from those preparations.

On August 6th 1966 a crowd of 60,000 left Parkhead excited and enraptured by a breathtaking display of exuberant, flowing football and finishing power as they administered a 4-1 thrashing to a Manchester United side containing the 'Holy Trinity' of Charlton, Law and Best, plus ex-Celt Pat Crerand, in a challenge match whose highlight for many in attendance was the sight of Jimmy Johnstone outshining United's golden boy, George Best, in itself a testament to Celtic's brimming confidence. It was their fifteenth consecutive match unbeaten in a run of 48 games (competitive and friendlies/challenge matches included) which would stretch from April 30th to December 24th 1966 before being broken by Dundee United's 3-2 Hogmanay victory at Tannadice. The Celtic juggernaut was taking on a frightful aspect, crushing opposing teams in its path, the likes of Clyde (6-0), St Mirren (8-2) and Dunfermline Athletic (6-3) left bewildered by their opponents' remorseless appetite for goals in their quest to retain the League Cup. Joe McBride netted 15 goals in his ten appearances in the competition, which was won for the second time in succession by Celtic in late October 1966, with the only goal of the final against Rangers being netted by Bobby Lennox with a slick 18th-minute finish to an Auld cross headed back by McBride across the goalmouth in an Old Firm contest during which the Celtic defence (undeservedly, a largely under-publicised sector of the team) was tested to its limits by the Ibrox men's relentless onslaught on Simpson's goal. The *Scottish Sunday Express* hailed this 21st successive victory in all competitions to date that season with a banner back page headline: "FOOTBALL KINGS OF ALL THEY SURVEY!".

The four clashes of the Glasgow giants would largely decide the destination of three trophies that season: the League Cup, the League Championship and the Glasgow Cup. Celtic's early ascendancy in these matches (prior to the League Cup triumph) was crucial to the momentum that Celtic were building in domestic competition. None of the spectators in the near 77,000 crowd could have left Ibrox Park on August 23rd 1966 unimpressed by the ruthless efficiency displayed by Celtic in their 4-0 Glasgow Cup first round victory. It was perhaps the most impressive indication to date of the effectiveness of Jock Stein's constant preaching to his players of the necessity to create space by drawing opponents out of position. To this end, he gave Charlie Gallagher, arguably the finest striker and passer of a ball in Scotland at the time, a wandering role designed to disrupt the home side's man-for-man marking policy by pulling full back Kai Johansen all over the place. The tactic had the desired effect, enabling Bobby Lennox in particular to use his electric pace and net a hat-trick by exploiting gaps in the Rangers rearguard, causing such havoc that Scottish international defenders John Greig and Ronnie McKinnon were hoisting distress signals long before the final whistle. Celtic went on to win the trophy without conceding a goal, achieving the same scoreline against both Queen's Park in the semi-final and Partick Thistle in the final. In the interim, Celtic inflicted another defeat (2-0) on their greatest rivals, with Auld and Murdoch, as they had done at Ibrox, taking a firm midfield grip in the league encounter at Parkhead on September 17th 1966, both even finding the time to net inside the first four minutes. The *Glasgow Herald* summed up the ruthless economy with which the home side won an unequal contest: "The hopeful upfield punt was the main weapon in their [Rangers] armoury and whereas they used the bludgeon, Celtic preferred the rapier."

European Cup, early rounds

With the advent of autumn, a Celtic squad bolstered by impressive runs to the 1964 and 1966 semi-finals of the European Cup-Winners' Cup was well placed to move forward on all fronts, but any notions that the club's debut in the European Cup on September 28th 1966 would be a smooth affair were to be jolted by the robust approach of the first round, first leg visitors FC Zurich, whose determination to keep the Scots at bay was not breached until the 64th minute, when the rumbustious Tommy Gemmell strode forward from his own half to run on to a John Clark crossfield pass and smash the ball high into the net from forty yards out. Five minutes later, Joe McBride further eased the tension that had earlier gripped the near 50,000 crowd with a low, 18-yard snapshot which appeared to be helped into the net by a deflection (2-0). Celtic were out of luck, however, when Danish referee Frede Hansen blew his whistle for time up just as a McBride header, a potential tie-clincher, was heading for the net.

Always keen to build up a file on potential future opponents, Inter Milan coach Helenio Herrera looked on as the 20,000 Swiss in the Letzigrund stadium on October 5th 1966 boomed out their pre-match optimism that their favourites would qualify for the next round, but Jock Stein was far from perturbed, saying that "I'm not naïve enough to think that I can take this team anywhere and win, but I honestly consider that if we strike a game at all, we won't lose." Celtic's defence drew the sting from the home side's early frenzied attacks before taking a 22nd minute lead through a Tommy Gemmell 30-yarder that totally deflated the Swiss. Fifteen minutes later, Steve Chalmers put the match (and the tie) to bed with a crisp finish to round off goalmouth pressure on the harassed defence following a Celtic corner. Shortly after the interval Tommy Gemmell ended the scoring (3-0, 5-0 on aggregate) with a cool conversion of a penalty award after Bobby Lennox, a menace throughout, was pulled down after outpacing two defenders.

Intriguingly, as the newspaper was quick to point out, the *Scottish Daily Mail's* horoscope on match day (Jock Stein's 44th birthday) read as follows: "LIBRA,

September 24-October 23: Big lift indicated in your affairs – something you have been working towards will suddenly take shape." That prediction was endorsed by FC Zurich player/coach Ladislav Kubala, who told a journalist friend, Leslie Vernon, that he would not be surprised to see the Scots carry off the trophy. Even this early, Celtic were being viewed as a team to be reckoned with. Or perhaps the outcome of Celtic's season had already been written in the stars…

Celtic's growing reputation as a worthy contender for European glory, a team well equipped to compete with the most exalted of clubs, went before them as they set out for their second round, first leg encounter. The fear factor had been in evidence in the headline reaction to the draw several weeks earlier in *L'Equipe* (France's top sporting newspaper): "Nantes will face the invincible Celtic." The Breton side became so preoccupied with Celtic's visit that they defied the French Football Federation by not allowing - as was their right at the time - any of their players to be fielded by the French national side in a European Nations' Cup qualifying match against Luxembourg (hardly a great footballing power) four days before the first leg. The French champions' coach José Arribas voiced his concern in a local newspaper, *Ouest France,* about a "pacy, virile, entirely efficient side" and stressed the necessity of restricting the space in which Celtic could manoeuvre. Jock Stein confounded him and the high hopes invested by the French nation in their side making a big impact in a competition, by springing a tactical surprise, playing Joe McBride, normally the spearhead of the attack, in a deep lying role, with Steve Chalmers enrolled as a front runner and striker and Jimmy Johnstone instructed to keep possession of the ball and take it deep into Nantes territory in order to take the pressure off the Celtic defence. The latter's extraordinary ball skills – feinting, weaving and twisting with the ball glued to his feet – entranced the 16,000 crowd at the rain-soaked Stade Marcel Saupin on November 30th 1966, prompting one French reporter to describe him as "a little redheaded lucky charm who looked as if he was barely out of school but who so tormented his immediate opponent De Michele with his pace, touch and dribbling as to be regarded as virtually unplayable."

Celtic had a dressing room scare shortly before kick-off when the prolific Joe McBride incurred the wrath of his manager by revealing his discovery that he had only brought along one boot. The striker was ordered to take a taxi back to the team's hotel, accompanied by assistant manager Sean Fallon. Fortunately, they found the missing boot, but on the return journey the taxi became snarled up in the traffic heading for the stadium, forcing the pair to get out and run the rest of the way to make it back in time. Bertie Auld concluded his revelation of this episode in the May 22nd 1992 edition of *The Sun* (Scottish edition) by saying that a raging Stein "let Joe know all about it", but the manager shouted his forgiveness to the player when, after Celtic were caught napping by an early (16th minute) opener for Nantes by Magny, they shrugged off the setback to draw level within ten minutes when McBride converted Lennox's cross with a powerful shot. Five minutes after the interval, Bobby Lennox edged Celtic in front with a close-in finish after latching on to a deft Murdoch pass and outpacing two defenders. Thereafter, Nantes appeared subdued by the threat of Celtic's pace and power, and their worst fears were confirmed in the 67th minute, when Budzinski's botched attempt at a clearance left Steve Chalmers with a virtual tap-in to make it 3-1 and enable Celtic to play out the remainder of the match in comfort. Allan Herron of the *Sunday Mail* captured the growing belief that Celtic were going places: "The Europeanisation of Celtic continues. They improve every time out. Step by step, little by little, they grow in stature as a force in the turbulent cross-tides of the European Cup." More recently, Herron, who covered all Celtic's matches in Europe that season, told co-author Pat Woods in an interview that it was "a fond memory and a real privilege" to travel with the club and witness a Scottish club gradually develop into European champions: "The players were essentially local boys who became a family, a bunch of friends who played together and looked out for each other. Then you had Jock Stein, the manager, a great listener who never stopped learning along the way, and Billy McNeill, the ideal leader on the park and the dressing-room link with the manager. I felt I was watching the cream of football."

A writer in the rival *Sunday Post* all but endorsed that verdict on December 4th 1966: "The first thing that strikes you as you join the Celtic party aboard their plane is their air of absolute confidence and faith in their own ability. This atmosphere never leaves you all the time you're with them." After highlighting Jock Stein's "success secrets" evident in Nantes - notably his meticulous and thorough preparation (including pacing out the length and breadth of pitches, checking their surface and that of the condition of the floodlighting) and leaving final instructions to players as late as possible - he cited the manager's statement of his supreme faith in his squad: "They've made a name for themselves in Europe. They've a perfect right to be confident. It's the greatest thing of all, provided it's channelled in the right direction." The writer concluded his piece as follows: "Can the 'wha's like us?' Celts win the European Cup this season? I'll tell you this - the team that beats them will have to be good. Very good."

The return leg at a rainswept Parkhead on December 7th 1966 before a near 40,000 crowd confirmed that Celtic had the playing resources (including seven international forwards) to match the increasing expectations of their fans. Without the services of the free-scoring Joe McBride, already suffering from the cartilage problem that would eventually rule him out for the rest of the season, it was indeed fortunate – or was it Jock Stein's intuition? - that on the day before the match the manager had signed what he described as "a complete forward line in one player" when the versatile Willie Wallace joined from Hearts for an estimated £30,000 fee, although he would not be eligible to play in the European Cup until the semi-finals stage. In the second leg, Celtic did not play with their now accustomed fluency, but were still able to overcome the over-elaborate visitors' offside tactics to run out 3-1 winners, advancing to the quarter-finals on a 6-2 aggregate. After only 13 minutes, Johnstone took advantage of a defensive lapse to run into the penalty box and beat the advancing keeper Castel with a low shot. Georgin gave Nantes hope of a revival with a first time shot from Blanchet's cross before the interval, but Steve Chalmers snuffed out French dreams in the 56th minute with a header from Johnstone's pinpoint cross, and Bobby Lennox rounded off the scoring by getting on the end of another Johnstone cross to toe the ball into the net. It was yet another of those competent, professional performances that were becoming Celtic's hallmark, and that on a night when Liverpool, one of the favourites to win the competition, were shredded 5-1 by Ajax in a foggy Amsterdam, notwithstanding which a shocked manager, Bill Shankly, made the astonishing claim that his side would "smash in seven in the return" (Ajax drew 2-2 at Anfield). In contrast, Celtic's chances were boosted by the Nantes forward, Jacques Simon, tipping them to win the tournament. Celtic were on a roll, gathering admirers on the way, and their supporters were daring to dream the impossible. The players, however, were kept firmly grounded: when asked by the *Scottish Sunday Express* in late 1966 about his prospects of creating a new goalscoring record in a single season for the club, that remorseless finisher Joe McBride politely declined, recognising that he would only risk losing his place in the team if he started to put himself first.

European Cup, Quarter-Finals

Earlier in that season Willie Waddell of the *Scottish Daily Express* had wondered, "Where is the team that can stand up to their [Celtic's] deadly efficiency?" Jock Stein had seen one in the shape of their quarter final opponents, a Yugoslav side called Vojvodina, whom the manager watched when they won their play-off at Real's Bernabeu stadium in the city of their opponents, Atlético Madrid, and had identified them as "a well drilled outfit that will push Celtic all the way", so much so that he confessed that he would have preferred to have drawn Atlético; he singled out the Slavs' huge goalkeeper, Pantelic, as outstanding in a team that came from two behind in the first six minutes of the play-off to win 3-2 after extra time. Vojvodina had already demonstrated the physical challenge that awaited the Scottish club, earning a reputation for toughness by having three players sent off during the previous two rounds, two of the dismissals (Trivic and Pusibrk, both forwards) coming in the Madrid play-off. Without those suspended forwards, the Slavs surely came to wish that the draw had scheduled the first leg for Celtic Park, where they would have been able to play two extra defenders and go all out to hold Celtic to at least a draw and then throw everything at the Scots in Novi Sad, where the suspended forwards would now have been available. After all, British clubs such as Manchester United, Rangers and Celtic had come to grief in Yugoslavia in recent seasons. Bobby Murdoch once told Pat Woods that he hated playing against sides from that region, since they were usually composed of tall, hard and technically well-equipped players: "You knew you were in a game", he added in that understated way of his.

Within a week of his return from the Spanish capital, Stein arranged for Dinamo Zagreb to come to Glasgow in early February to give his players a taste of what they might expect against Dinamo's compatriots, an experiment which had mixed results, with the visitors winning 1-0. In the first leg at the Gradski Stadion in Novi Sad on March 1st 1967, Celtic, with the majestic McNeill's blond head "sweeping the penalty area and beyond like radar" in the same fashion as Allan Herron had watched him, as a raw youngster, winning every ball in the air for junior club Blantyre Victoria ten years earlier, Celtic's tightness in defence was frustrating the home side to the point of despair before the roof fell in with twenty minutes remaining. Tommy Gemmell's faulty passback led to the lively Stanic netting the only goal of the match. In public at least, Jock Stein was philosophical about the defeat, stating that his team had been unlucky to lose – and that by the narrowest of margins – but he added, prophetically, that he "felt like kicking Tommy Gemmell's backside for that stupid mistake, but he has seen us through with great goals before now... and he will do the same again."

He would also have drawn some comfort, albeit indirectly, had he known that on that same evening the Inter Milan coach, Helenio Herrera, had told a press conference after their 2-0 away victory over Real Madrid (3-0) on aggregate, that he saw Celtic as the only serious rivals left for his team to face in the competition, though there was a suspicion that he may have been paying lip service to the impact that the Scots had already made that season. If his statement sounded a touch patronizing, the Milan-based *Supersport* magazine felt no need for equivocation about the destination of the European Cup, its front cover being emblazoned with the headline "Inter Coppa No. 3." The *Nerazzurri* had by now developed a proprietorial attitude to the trophy, leading Herrera to claim before and after the final in Lisbon that his club had a "moral entitlement" to the trophy, having had the "harder" route to the *Estádio Nacional*, a questionable assertion. The draw for the first round had not paired Inter with fearsome opponents in Torpedo Moscow, a side making their (and the Soviet

Union's) debut in the competition, and yet Dinamo lost out only to an away goal in the San Siro stadium, having being denied an early goal when the referee (Kurt Tschenscher, the West German who refereed the Lisbon final) did not agree with their claims that a Brednev shot had crossed the line after coming down off the crossbar. Inter were accused of anti-football tactics, including time-wasting, to achieve their passage to the next round with a 0-0 draw. Their progress to the quarter finals was secured more impressively with home and away victories (4-1 on aggregate) over Vasas Budapest, the result of Inter's counter-attacking exploiting the Hungarian side's naivety. It would have been interesting to see how the Italians would have coped with Vojvodina.

The Vojvodina coach, Vujadin Boskov, could not hide his disappointment about the failure of his players to travel to Scotland with a more substantial lead, in contrast to the scenes of jubilation which had marked the first leg triumph. Geoffrey Green, in his report for *The Times* of London, had noted the crowd's reaction to Stanic's goal, celebrating as if the tie was over: "From that moment on bonfires were burning on the terraces. That is the Slav way of expressing victory. Up the [floodlight] pylons, too, there were crowds of Yugoslav supporters. There were klaxons and rockets emerging from the great crowd [of around 25,000] with velour hats, caps and berets." In their view it was lift-off to the semi-finals, and in the first half of the return leg on March 8th 1967 Celtic's performance did little to suggest that a rather predictable home side could knock the fast-tackling, tight-marking Slavs off course. The visitors, indeed, could have put the tie beyond their opponents' reach had Pusibrk and Radosav not squandered two close-in chances.

During the interval at a fretful Parkhead, Stein emphasised to his players that they had to get a grip in midfield, where he said that Vojvodina were getting too much space and time in which to manouevre. He also made a couple of tactical adjustments designed to give the visitors food for thought, which proved sufficiently disruptive to Vojvodina's composure as to enable Celtic, who gradually upped the pace early in the second half, to draw level on aggregate on the hour mark, albeit only as a result of a howler by the hitherto solid if somewhat exhibitionistic keeper Pantelic, who failed to deal with Gemmell's low cross, allowing the ever-alert Steve Chalmers to net from close in.

Thereafter, Celtic - driven on by a near 70,000 crowd - went all out for the winner, but as the Slavs held out grimly even the Celtic bench was becoming resigned to a play-off (in Rotterdam a week later) as the match entered the last few minutes. Then, drama as Celtic were awarded yet another corner. Billy McNeill takes up the story: "I knew that Charlie Gallagher was going to put over a long corner when I saw two defenders run out to cover Jimmy Johnstone at the flag. I had been coming up for all the corners, but hadn't got my head to any of them. The keeper was always there first to punch the ball away. But he was a fraction late coming out this time and I knew somehow the ball was mine. Charlie doesn't float his crosses. He hits them and, if you connect, the ball goes like a rocket." For his part, Gallagher told one interviewer (David Allister) that "when the Yugoslav defenders raced out of the box to cover Johnstone I knew it had to be a long kick, and I saw Billy on the edge of the 18 yard line" (*Scottish Daily Express*, March 10th 1967). The "golden head" of the Celtic skipper arced the ball firmly over a defender striving frantically on the goalline to keep the ball from entering the roof of the net.

Someone in the press box timed the goal which took Celtic through to the semi-finals as having come at 47 seconds from the final whistle, and David Allister claimed it was the fifth time (four of them in Cup ties, most notably this match and the 1965 Scottish Cup Final) that the Gallagher-McNeill partnership had combined to net a decider. McNeill's winner set off celebrations at Celtic Park the likes of which have rarely been seen since. Jock Stein was quick to sing the praises of the "greatest fans in Britain" who had willed the team to victory, adding that "It was almost as if they were on the park – extra arms... extra legs... extra courage." The goal's significance was not lost on the home eleven, as Ronnie Simpson later recalled: "From that moment on we knew we could do it", while John Clark would describe "the sheer drama and the ear-splitting noise created by 75,000 Celtic fans that evening" as his highlight of the journey to Lisbon.

The training ground, where Jock Stein had placed great emphasis on 'dead ball' situations, had come up trumps again, leaving a downcast Boskov to nod ruefully that "Celtic fought like mountain lions, the McNeill goal was like being hit by an earthquake." One theologically-inclined home supporter, it seemed, had been taking no chances with the outcome. John McLauchlan, then a six-year-old in the early stages of his initiation into the Celtic family and whose match ticket had been tucked into a birthday card two days earlier, told co-author Pat Woods that he had become aware from relatives' conversations that the club might be on the verge of a hugely significant achievement. He recalled making his way with his father, Willie, after the final whistle through the delirious throngs down Kerrydale Street and on to London Road, the atmospheric glow from the four steepling floodlight pylons illuminating the surroundings on a "dark, dismal, rainy night", when suddenly a friend of his father, Denis McEneny (the owner of *The Glen Bar* in Rutherglen) appeared at their side and said "I had the rosary out there, Willie", to which the latter, noting Denis's rosary beads still wrapped round his right knuckle, replied: "I can see, Denis, that you still have your rosary out - I think we were all praying in there tonight."

Looking back a quarter of a century later, Steve Chalmers would view the dramatic late winner as a product of the manager's gift for psychology in respect of planting the seeds of the squad's confidence and ambition: "Before every important match that season the 'Big Man' always told us this could prove to be an exceptional season, and as we won every competition we entered, sweeping all before us, we realized he could well prove to be right." Ken Jones, writing in the London edition of the *Daily Mirror*, was, however, sceptical, if not insulting, about the Scots' chances of attaining such heights: "Celtic are through to the semi-finals of the European Cup – but they may not be good enough to win it. With not a shade of green in sight and Glasgow once again a good 400 miles away, I feel safe to make a statement that would have been the blood brother to an insult at Parkhead on Wednesday. And I do mean blood! Celtic - if you haven't heard – play there beneath a banner of the Irish Republic and to the occasional accompaniment of its anthem. They are followed by a public whose devotion is fierce, who nominate the Pope as their unofficial patron and manager Jock Stein as the greatest magician since Merlin." There is an element of disdain about his description of Stein as "a weaver of dreams" and his reference to a popular parody of a television jingle advertising Heinz beans, "A million housewives every day/ Pick up their rosaries and say/ Stein, Stein, Stein." He concluded by stating that he would hate to be in Glasgow on the night Celtic's dreams were broken, as he suspected they would be, for "I do not regard Celtic as good enough to achieve what none of the top Football League clubs has accomplished", adding that he would not grudge the fans success if it derived from "the drug that cures all the worrying ills of living" (March 10th 1967).

European Cup, Semi-Finals

Jones' prediction was looking uncomfortably close to fulfilment during the early stages of the next test of Celtic's European credentials, for there was an eerie familiarity about the semi-final first leg with Dukla Prague, seasoned campaigners in Europe, on April 12th 1967, as the first half drew to a close. The near 75,000 crowd at Parkhead had the same distinctly uneasy feeling as had pervaded the ground for much of the Vojvodina match, particularly after Dukla Prague made it 1-1 through Strunc, the result of the Celtic defence having been thrown into disarray in the 44th minute by a typically decisive incursion by the legendary playmaker Josef Masopust. The Czechs had thus cancelled out Jimmy Johnstone's opener on the half-hour mark when he had dinked the ball over the outrushing Viktor. Once again Jock Stein was on hand to provide reassurance to a side which had displayed a touch of nervousness. "Just his presence seemed to achieve something in itself", Ronnie Simpson once said of Stein in his pomp. Stein told his players that there was no need to panic, just "wear them down with your pressure was the basic message." The Czechs had entered their dressing room at the interval delighted to have contained the running power of Celtic, but emerged from it to discover, much to their consternation, that within a matter of minutes the home side was turning the screw even more relentlessly. It all became too much for the visitors, who cracked in the last half hour. Willie Wallace, declared ineligible for the quarter-final tie against Vojvodina by UEFA's qualifying rules despite having been signed in early December, now came into his own. In the space of six minutes before the halfway mark in the second half he swung the tie decisively in Celtic's favour. He edged Celtic in front by running on to a long ball downfield by Tommy Gemmell, judging its flight perfectly before cleverly lobbing it over Viktor, then blasting a 20-yarder which left the keeper helpless after the cunning Bertie Auld, a master of feinting, initially pretended to re-place the ball, then suddenly tapped the free kick aside to Wallace. It was left to Desmond Hackett in the London edition of the *Daily Express* to deliver his verdict on the damage inflicted by Celtic's lightning strikes on a Czech side which had toiled to keep the margin of defeat down to two goals (3-1): "Leaden legged with the strain of combat, ruthlessly dazed and destroyed."

The referee, Joaquim Campos of Portugal, who had refereed the Glasgow club's match in Nantes and seen all the top European sides in action, was greatly impressed by Celtic's performance, stating that their pace and stamina was unmatched. These comments (along with others which he had made in the Portuguese press in the autumn) added him to the list of those who envisioned the Glasgow side winning the cup, joining Zurich's coach Kubala, Jacques Simon of Nantes, and Vojvodina's coach Boskov. "You can't live against play like that", said Campos, "even Inter Milan will be stretched." And now 'Lisbon fever' was growing apace. The following morning, Kathleen McGinley, of Holiday Enterprises, a travel agency of the Partick area of Glasgow, arrived at the premises to find a long line of people waiting outside to book trips to the final. She told the *Daily Record* that the agency had booked three planeloads before the first leg and "now my husband Jim has gone to London to try to book more aircraft." Jock Stein, however, believed that all this optimism about Celtic's prospects had to be tempered with a degree of caution, not just because of the club's commitments in the Scottish Cup (a final against Aberdeen due to take place just a few days after their return from Prague) and in the final stretch of the League championship (with Rangers still challenging strongly) but also out of concern about Dukla's thirst for revenge. The great Masopust was still contending four decades later that the team he captained did not deserve to lose in Glasgow, stating that two of Celtic's goals were lucky, although he did concede that the uniqueness of Jimmy Johnstone (the 'Flying Flea', as he called him) had made a significant contribution to Dukla's defeat: "He was amazing. We occasionally played man-to-man marking, and we tried it against him. It didn't work. He did things no-one expected." He would not be the first – or last – to pay homage to the phenomenon that was 'Jinky'."

Celtic returned the compliment on a chilly afternoon in Prague, with Willie Wallace being deployed to shadow Masopust in the Stadion Juliska on April 25th 1967 in front of a near 20,000 crowd which featured a large contingent of heavy-coated men in uniform (Dukla being the army club). There has been a bit of a debate over the years about Stein's tactics in this second leg, a controversy of sorts fuelled by players differing in print over the instructions imparted to them. The manager himself was adamant on the matter in his comments in the *Celtic Football Guide*, Season 1967–68: "I have regrets that we were forced into such a style, but I make no apologies for asking the team to become completely defensive. The pressure of fixtures was really building up at the time." He was essentially confirming his captain Billy McNeill's statement in Glasgow's *Evening Citizen* on the day after the match to the effect that the tactic had been laid down at Seamill, Celtic's favourite venue for pre-match preparations for the big occasion, and had been arrived at after the players had their say. Wallace, said McNeill, had carried out his assignment to perfection: "He pushed Masopust further and further back into his own defence to pick up the ball before he [Masopust] could turn about and then think about attack-building. By then we were all organised to meet whatever was coming. It all worked so nicely that the Czechs had to try to pierce us with the long shot or the lofted pass. We were able to pick off this type of game." Vacenovsky's early squandering of a good chance, wildly slicing a shot so badly that it ran out for a throw-in to Celtic, was symptomatic of Dukla's hurried finishing after laborious and slow build-up play, while their constant hitting of high balls from the wings into the Scots' goalmouth, where goalkeeper Simpson and centre-half McNeill in particular dealt with them fairly comfortably, played right into the hands of the visitors. As the match petered out in a 0-0 draw (a 3-1 aggregate victory to Celtic) several Dukla players were seen to have their stockings dragging around their ankles and their spirits were flagging perceptibly, signalling another victory for the away side's (now) renowned stamina and gritty determination. The Czech sports magazine *Stadión*'s verdict carried a front page headline which had overtones of irony with regard to the final: "Lisbon disappeared because of the Scottish wall!" Little wonder that Jock Stein was always uncomfortable when that match was discussed.

When the Celtic party arrived back in Glasgow that evening, they were greeted with choruses of *The Celtic Song* by supporters who had packed the airport. As the Celtic party made its way through milling crowds overjoyed by their favourites having made history by becoming the first British club to reach the final, Bobby Lennox summed up the feelings of everyone connected with Celtic when he told a reporter that "it's a wonderful feeling to be in the European Cup Final", while trainer Neil Mochan went one further by insisting "We will win it – easy." For some months the refrain of *We're on our way to Lisbon, We shall not be moved* had rung around Celtic Park. Now it had become a reality. A legend was in the making.

CHAPTER 4
In the Groove

Celtic now had to put aside thoughts of Lisbon, though of course, that was well nigh impossible, but they gave every indication of being fully focused on their remaining targets when they inflicted a 2-0 defeat on Aberdeen in the final of April 29th 1967 to add the Scottish Cup to the League Cup and the Glasgow Cup in their quest for a clean sweep. Willie Wallace's brace underlined what an invaluable asset he had become since being snatched from under the noses of Rangers four months earlier. The eleven who became known as 'The Lisbon Lions' had first come together for a 4-0 League victory against St Johnstone at Perth on January 14th 1967, and it was a line-up that seems to have grown on Jock Stein as the season drew to a close. It was certainly a blend which was displaying its capacity to come up trumps on the big occasion, no matter the challenge. Fresh from the backs-to-the-wall display in Prague which had carried the club through to the European Cup final, they demonstrated a killer instinct at Hampden Park that bore the hallmark of a team enveloped in unshakeable self-confidence. Celtic struck, cobra-like, on either side of the interval to kill off Aberdeen's hope of taking the trophy back north for the first time in twenty years. Three minutes before half-time, Bobby Lennox resisted any temptation to swing a corner kick into the goalmouth where Billy McNeill's aerial presence was already prominent, opting instead for a short pass to Bertie Auld, then gathering the return to elude two defenders before driving the ball low and hard across the box, where the predatory Willie Wallace jabbed it past goalkeeper Clark. Four minutes after the break the latter was again left bewildered by the suddenness of it all when Jimmy Johnstone carried on a Bobby Murdoch/Steve Chalmers move by scuttling to the bye-line before cutting the ball back to the remorselessly efficient Wallace, who crashed it high into the net from some ten yards out.

Three down, two to go. However, four days later those who were predicting a procession to a clean sweep of the domestic trophies were given a severe jolt when Dundee United, Celtic's Scottish nemesis that season, defied the odds by twice coming from behind at Parkhead to beat Celtic 3-2 for the second time that season and revive Rangers' hopes of snatching the league title. The scene was set for a dramatic climax at Ibrox Park three days later. Victory for the 'Light Blues' in this, their final league match of the season, would edge them a point in front of their greatest rivals, who would then have to take at least a point in the remaining (home) fixture against Kilmarnock ten days before the European Cup final. Celtic went into this contest with a superior goal average, but also in the knowledge that the club had not won successive championships since 1917. And there would be two famous guests, both spies you might say, in attendance on May 6th 1967.

Helenio Herrera, the Inter Milan coach, accompanied by the sons (Gian Marco and Massimo) of the club's president, Angelo Moratti, flew to Glasgow in a four-seater private jet loaned by Giovanni Borghi, a friend of Herrera and the Inter president who was the head of Ignis, a Varese-based household appliances company. Their arrival upstaged even that of film star Sean Connery (aka '007', James Bond), who had flown up from London by scheduled flight and found out, for once, that he was not the cynosure of press attention when their planes touched down almost simultaneously. (There was, of course, also a Celtic connection with the superstar actor: three weeks later, while in Rome to promote his latest Bond movie *You Only Live Twice*, he was not interested in discussing the film with an interviewer sent by the illustrated news weekly *Domenica del Corriere*, preferring instead to enthuse about the European Cup final, which he had watched on television while in the city and, more particularly, Jock Stein, to whom he had sent a telegram of congratulations in which he described the Celtic manager as "the pride of the Scottish race." Such was his admiration for Stein that he told the interviewer "There's a touch of the magician about him, you know.")

That other magician, Herrera, would depart Ibrox with plenty of food for thought during the two-hour flight back to Italy (more specifically Turin) to prepare for his team's crucial championship match the following day with Juventus in the *Derby d'Italia*, so called because of the bitterness of the rivalry. On a miserable Glasgow day of pitiless, driving rain which made the pitch resemble "a paddy field in a monsoon", he and 78,000 others had to be impressed by Celtic's stamina, pace and resolve as they battled to a 2-2 finish against their greatest rivals which clinched the club's first ever Scottish treble (League Cup, Scottish Cup and League title) thanks in no small measure to the tenacity of Jimmy Johnstone, who was on hand after Lennox's shot hit a post to net an equaliser which prevented Rangers going in at the interval with the psychological boost of being in front after Jardine's spectacular opener. Then the little redhead put Celtic ahead in the 74th minute, receiving a Steve Chalmers throw-in before veering inside to evade McKinnon and, before he could be closed down, arrowed a magnificent 25-yarder into the roof of the net. Rangers, gritty as always, salvaged a draw with a Hynd counter ten minutes from time. Celtic's equally resolute display was yet further testament to a team spirit second to none. In an interview he gave shortly after attending the European Cup final in Lisbon, the striker Joe McBride recalled that, after returning to Celtic Park following the March 1967 cartilage operation which ruled him out for the rest of the season, he had noticed the mounting tension as Celtic chased the dream of a clean sweep of the domestic and European honours, with both the League Cup and Glasgow Cup already in the boardroom: "No wonder the strain was beginning to show. Most players tried to hide it. But, knowing them so well, I could tell the difference." During the early months of the year, some Celtic players had struggled for fitness – Jimmy Johnstone was on and off with colds and chills, Bobby Lennox had muscle trouble, Bobby Murdoch was carrying a long-term ankle injury that never fully healed – but had refused to bend the knee. Intriguingly too, in an interview with *France Football* after the Vojvodina tie, Jock Stein had expressed fears for the tiredness of his team after a hard season to date. Clearly, however, as they went on to demonstrate, here was a team prepared, in every sense, to go the proverbial extra mile.

Gian Maria Gazzaniga, in the special wrap-around supplement to Milan's *Il Giorno* published on the day of the European Cup final, recalled Herrera as saying the following after his Ibrox spy mission: "Celtic is a really formidable side. No one has a set role. They all keep switching, seven defending, seven attacking. They are the strongest team that this season's European Cup has thrown up." Sincere or not, the comments surely also reflected his concerns about the sudden and alarming lack of conviction being displayed by his own side. After ejecting Real Madrid from the European Cup with an imperious display in the second leg of the quarter finals in Madrid (2- 0, 3-0 on aggregate), Inter were described by the correspondent of *France Football* as "a team with nerves of steel, an infallible machine which dictated the outcome of the match the other night like no previous opponent in European contests at the Bernabeu, reducing the Cup holders to impotence." Seven weeks later, after watching Inter fail to beat ten-man CSKA Sofia, reputedly the easy draw of the semi finals, in the first leg at the San Siro, the watching BBC commentator Kenneth Wolstenholme concluded that Inter looked "a very worried team, more worried than I have seen them before, including their two previous [and victorious] European Cup Finals."

Another 1-1 draw in Sofia brought the necessity for a play-off on May 3rd

1967 which was originally scheduled for Graz. Already wary of the reaction there to their [CSKA's] criticism of the first leg's Austrian referee (Wlachojanis), a man who had also upset Celtic three years earlier with his apparent favouritism to MTK Budapest as the Glasgow side went down to a 3-4 aggregate defeat in the European Cup Winners Cup semi-finals, the Bulgarians succumbed to the lure of western currency and agreed to Inter's proposal that the venue for the play-off be changed to Bologna, in Italy. Financially, Inter's offer of a two-thirds share of the gate receipts was "a fabulous piece of business", in the words of the German magazine *Sports Illustrierte*, which also noted that CSKA again fell foul of a referee (Dienst of Switzerland) who "let all objectivity pass by and set himself up against the Bulgarians from the very start", apparently threatening to send off their players for the most innocuous of fouls "whilst paying no attention to the Italian players who pulled the legs from under their opponents." Inter, virtually playing at home despite a 7,000 shortage in their fans' take-up of tickets, squeaked through 1-0 to the final, but with them now also shipping points in the title race with Juventus, their supporters were now asking questions of Herrera's management of a hitherto "terrifying war machine" which many of them now feared had reached the end of the road, a waning of confidence also suggested by the attendance in Bologna.

It was against this backdrop that Jock Stein travelled to Turin to see Inter playing Juventus on the day following the title decider at Ibrox. When he met Helenio Herrera by arrangement at the Hotel Ambasciatori in Turin before the match, he found him to be a polite and co-operative figure who observed the usual courtesies and formalities which generally took place on such occasions, with the Inter coach assuring his Scottish counterpart that transport would be provided to the *Stadio Comunale* and a match ticket made available. One can only imagine Stein's anger an hour or so later when he and an accompanying journalist, John Mackenzie of the *Scottish Daily Express*, stood on the hotel steps and watched the Inter Milan team bus disappear around the corner, necessitating a taxi journey to the stadium and access to the ground by means of Mackenzie's press ticket plus "a fair amount of bluff and brass neck", as the latter described it in an article three years later. Stein felt better as he watched the home side turn up the title pressure on Inter with a 1-0 victory and, surprisingly for a normally circumspect manager, was happy to observe to the Italian press that "Inter seemed tired, which would be our good fortune" and had "committed the error of playing for a draw", adding that although Inter had more experience than Celtic at the highest level, his team had "more rhythm and can run for 90 minutes, a capacity which Inter's players don't seem to have", all clear jibes at Herrera. More pointedly, he gave the impression of a man without a care in the world, having concluded that his tactic in the European Cup final would be to keep his players busy, keep them running and turning a Milanese side feeling the tide of opprobrium being directed towards the club by their fellow countrymen, as illustrated by two incidents that had taken place just before the match between Italy's two most powerful clubs at the time.

Gianmarco and Massimo Moratti, the sons of the Inter president, were the target of booing and vile abuse by Juventus fans at the stadium entrance, while the Inter captain, Armando Picchi, reacted to the hostility of the home supporters when the Inter bus drew up outside the ground by brandishing a 1,000 *lire* banknote at them, which was taken as a clear (and insulting) reminder of the much publicised wealth enjoyed by a club bankrolled by oil magnate Angelo Moratti, a situation much resented by the rest of Italian football, which suspected that it enabled Inter to have too much influence in the game, particularly in the case of refereeing appointments. Herrera once responded to the hostility with a comment on his club's European campaigns, "If we win, we win for Italy – if we lose, we lose for Inter."

Mackenzie would later describe the Turin episode as one in which the first shots had been fired in the war of nerves which preceded Celtic's Lisbon triumph. In the days leading up to that match, Stein would insist that "Herrera and I are just the men behind the scenes, the game is played by 22 players – 11 in green and white and 11 in blue and black", but in truth it had become highly personal. Stein left Turin not only convinced that Celtic would win the European Cup, but he was also set on revenge for the deliberate slights he had endured that day, including his last sight of Herrera at the hotel, backslapping the Scot with "a glint of a smile on his face" which left Stein with the distinct impression that he was being patronized, judging it to be yet another of Herrera's exercises in one-upmanship which had started the day before, when *Il Mago*'s promise of a lift to Turin in the private jet did not materialize because of the small size of the plane which accommodated the Inter president's two sons at the expense of the Celtic manager. Herrera's explanation to pressmen took the form of a calculated insult: "Mr Stein is a big man – too big to get in. It would have not been comfortable." The meeting in Lisbon of these two highly-charged, driven men – the flamboyant, voluble Herrera and the dour, rather laconic Stein - promised to be highly combustible. After all, two could play at Herrera's mind games.

CHAPTER 5
Two of a Kind?

It would become a night heavy in premonitions, that night of October 9th 1963 when – if you believe in serendipity – the stars were aligning in such a way as to set in motion Celtic's finest hour. There he was, the consummate professional, snugly ensconced in the sitting room of his well-appointed Via Domenichino flat in Milan, a room 'walled' by shelves containing files of newspaper cuttings and meticulously prepared dossiers on football, and the place where he was focusing his attention on potential future European Cup opponents via the medium of television, yet feeling sufficiently relaxed as to give his wife María Morilla (according to the Portuguese society magazine *Flama*, a supporter of Atlético Madrid) a running commentary on the second leg of the tie between her club's city rivals Real Madrid and Rangers which resulted in a 6–0 victory (7–0 on aggregate) for the *madrileños* in front of an 85,000 Bernabeu crowd that he thought should have been 10–0.

Unwittingly, however, the seeds of his own downfall were being sown as Inter Milan coach Helenio Herrera watched the aforementioned debacle unfold on a night when an 8,000 crowd at Celtic Park, huddling from the misery of gale force winds and torrential rain in the stand and 'Jungle' enclosure, could not have conceived of future glory in a sunny Lisbon as they watched the men in green and white cruise to a 5-0 European Cup-Winners' Cup win (10–1 on aggregate) over a mediocre Basel side, a performance which could not quite dispel the sense of crisis (only thunder and lightning were needed to complete the backdrop) which had enshrouded an arena plunged into gloom since the opening day of the season by the 'achievement' of only one victory in their first six League matches and an early exit from the League Cup – while, most irritatingly of all, during that period Rangers had won the three 'Old Firm' fixtures, two in the League Cup section and one in the League. In addition, of course, six long years had elapsed since Celtic had won a major trophy.

There was no disguising the self-satisfaction which prevailed at Ibrox Park while Rangers' domestic hegemony seemed unchallengeable, but their limitations in the wider sphere, in which they had played thirty-four matches in European competition compared to Celtic's four, could no longer be overlooked. Certainly the *Scottish Daily Express* thought so, prompting the newspaper to posit the notion that Scottish football needed a revolution. To this end, it sent a reporter, George Reid, to interview the man it styled "the world's greatest soccer coach", whose thoughts were duly published in a three-part series in mid-October 1963 entitled 'Challenge to Scots soccer'. Herrera identified three areas which demanded particular attention if its "amateurishness" was to be erased: discipline – the need for an absolute dictator ("When I say 'do this', the players do it") ; trainers/coaches – "They themselves need to be trained", and "There is too much training without the ball, too much running about", e.g. monotonous lapping of the track); and tactical deficiencies – "the manager/ coach who is surprised by the other team's tactics is defeated already", citing as an example the zonal marking employed by Rangers which left gaps for di Stéfano and Puskas to exploit). Gair Henderson of Glasgow's *Evening Times* had already underlined the latter point by castigating Rangers, a notoriously conservative club in football matters, for not spying on their opponents, or indeed making any detailed planning, before their tie against the record European Cup holders. At the end of the series Herrera issued a front page invitation to managers of Scottish clubs to come to Milan to study his methods, an offer taken up by two of the more famous personalities of a small country's native game, namely Willie Waddell and Jock Stein, respectively managers of Kilmarnock and Dunfermline.

Despite their differences in temperament and personality, the cosmopolitan Helenio Herrera and the quintessentially dour Scot Jock Stein were essentially kindred spirits in their passion for football. 'Lisbon Lion' Jim Craig, when asked in 2002 to sum up Jock Stein in twenty words or less, described his former boss as follows: "Strong in character, charismatic, thoughtful, intelligent, tactically aware, knowledgeable, organized, single-minded, difficult to please, ruthless and ambitious." It could just as well have been a pen portrait of Herrera, who shared a reputation with Stein of being a bad loser. It is ironic, therefore, to reflect that their historic clash in Lisbon might never have taken place. When appointed manager of Inter in 1960, Herrera had boasted at his first press conference: "Give me three years and we will be champions of Italy, Europe and the world!" A mere two (barren) years into his stewardship his future had been already the focus of speculation following a doping 'scandal' at Inter, the handling of which created a rift in the relationship between Herrera and Moratti, a President frustrated by the club's failure to break the Juventus/ AC Milan domination of the championship. This state of affairs left the coach feeling unsettled as he set off to take charge of Spain in the World Cup finals being held in Chile. Meantime, *MilanInter*, a newspaper which covered the doings of both the Milan giants, stated that several sources in Spain were "insistent" that Herrera was set to join Atlético Bilbao. The move did not take place, a significant factor apparently being the backing he was given by the Inter fans that summer.

However, he made himself a hostage to fortune in the opening phase of season 1962-63, when Inter accrued only seven points from the same number of league matches, and he was well aware that the President was intent on change, with an approach having already been made to Edmondo Fabbri, who had recently guided modest Mantova through three divisions to Serie 'A', a meteoric rise during which one journalist dubbed the team *Piccolo Brasile* ('Little Brazil') on account of a creative, attacking style of play that was the antithesis of Inter's. Herrera, still backed by the fans, who displayed banners at the San Siro warning Moratti that they still had faith in Herrera, would survive, but the corner was only really turned after a "clear the air" meeting following a second league defeat that season at the hands of unfashionable Atalanta, this time at Bergamo in early March 1963. On the club's return to Milan, an embarrassed President, in an atmosphere where it was said that "you could hear a pin drop", proceeded to tear a strip off the playing and backroom staff, including Herrera, for whom there appeared to be lukewarm backing in the ranks. However, the coach appears to have got the message that there was no future for him at the club if he did not deliver soon. A 6-0 home victory over Genoa the following weekend steadied the ship and paved the road for the club's first league title since 1954. The legend of *La Grande Inter* was born, following up that breakthrough by achieving the unique feat of lifting both the European Cup and World Club Championship in two successive seasons. As for Fabbri (who went on to become the Italian national coach), his reputation plummeted when Italy exited from the 1966 World Cup finals after a humiliating defeat at the hands of North Korea.

During the trip (sponsored by the *Scottish Daily Express*) to view Herrera's methods in late 1963, Stein, who had guided Dunfermline Athletic to a Scottish Cup final triumph over Celtic in 1961 and turned them into a team to be reckoned with in European competition, described Herrera after their first meeting as "an infectious wee devil" and a man "with a single mindedness and driving urge to get the best out of his players". In addition to absorbing Herrera's philosophy in regard to autocracy and tactical approach, Stein admitted that the Argentinian's training programs had been an eye-opener, citing also the additional advantage of mixing with people of Herrera's standing in the game, namely that after being in this sort of company "something was bound to rub off on your players – if nothing else, it helps their morale and boosts their confidence." He would make no bones, however, about his opposition to Herrera's win-at-all-costs philosophy as expressed in his favouring *catenaccio*, as Stein explained to *France Football* in May 1967: "Defensive tactics are ruining the image of football. This game was not invented for the purpose of avoiding defeat." He had no time for what he regarded as "automated football." An inflexible style of play which left little or no scope for improvisation would inevitably go awry, Stein believed, using the analogy that a machine cannot think. By its very definition, *catenaccio* has a tendency to be boring, and it was an article of faith for Stein that spectators must be given value for money. Not for nothing would he demand that his players go out and win the European Cup with style.

All things considered, as Waddell observed, the experience had broadened both their horizons and Stein, in particular, had learned from Herrera that "the best work of a manager is done not on Saturdays or match days and the telling factor is the application to detail everyday of the week, every minute of the working day." Another insight for Stein into the minutiae of the game to be absorbed by a man who delighted in hoovering up football knowledge, and an observation which chimed with his ambition to reach the pinnacle of his profession. Both Stein and Herrera were obsessive about the game, to the point that they virtually lived football twenty-four hours a day. Douglas Ritchie of *The Sun* (Scottish Edition) stated that he had seen Jock Stein going for two days and nights without sleep before a big match on the Continent, "his mind so keyed up that he just wouldn't close his eyes" (May 18th 1967). Football became all-consuming for them both from the moment they started kicking a ball for fun in their childhood; and both considered themselves journeymen players (Herrera even described his performances as a professional player as "a disgrace") before compensating for their deficiencies by becoming students of the game. Herrera's rationalisation was identical to Stein's, the former stating that "the greats are too good to have to train hard, for if you can do something naturally because it comes to you instinctively, it is difficult to teach someone else how to do it." Herrera adopted a more formal approach, earning a coaching diploma whilst playing in wartime occupied France, where he won the Coupe de France with Racing Club de Paris in 1942 before taking charge at Puteaux and Stade Français, then progressing to becoming *entraîneur* or *préparateur physique* (the equivalent of the British trainer, with perhaps some coaching or technical input) to the French national side, a position in which he first came to the attention of the press on this side of the Channel when 'Waverley' (W.G. Gallacher) of the *Daily Record* quoted the "French team trainer Monsieur Herrera" as saying "we must win our first victory over Scotland, our team is in grand physical condition" (May 22nd 1948). Even this early in his non-playing career he was clearly not lacking in self-belief, for the home side won the challenge match 3-0.

Herrera's coaching career would take him to Spain and Portugal before taking on the prestigious post at CF Barcelona in the late 1950s. Even winning the Championship there would not save him from the wrath of the fans when he failed to stop their hated rivals Real Madrid winning home and away in the 1960 European Cup semi-finals en route to their fifth successive triumph in the competition. Angelo Moratti, the president of Inter Milan, who had engaged ten unsuccessful coaches (a couple of whom did two stints) during his first five years at the helm, eventually struck it lucky by hiring Herrera on the rebound, as it were. Herrera, operating alongside Moratti as the twin shapers of *La Grande Inter*, would earn a reputation as an innovative coach, becoming possibly the first to combine the technical, medical, dietary and psychological aspects of management which have come to be accepted as the norm in the modern game. Sandro Mazzola, one of the most notable players to prosper under Herrera's methods, would claim that Herrera was ahead of his time with his philosophy of "First I train your mind, then I train your body." His overriding motto was that the result is everything (he was quoted in a German biography, published in 1967, as saying "I'm paid to win, not to play nicely as well"), and he had no scruples about achieving success by taking full control of his playing squad, which included the monitoring of their private lives. When one interviewer asked him where entertainment came in his priorities, Herrera looked at him "as if he had spoken in some unheard of language" and he would doubtless have pointed to the trophies he accumulated in his eight years at Inter Milan (three League titles, two European Cups and two World Championships) as vindication of his methods. It was a record which he would have regarded as ample justification for him becoming the highest paid coach in world football. He signed a new contract for season 1965-66 worth a guaranteed £57,000 to retain his services at a time when CF Barcelona tried to tempt him and his midfield general, Luis Suárez, back to the Camp Nou.

An egocentric, divisive figure notorious for his ungraciousness to opponents and possessing an overpowering self-confidence which enabled him to revel in the tag of Europe's finest coach, the 'King of the blackboard' brooked no contradiction, shrugging off complaints that he had created a war machine which too often ground out results that the more partisan Inter fans applauded but which left the rest of football disgusted. For all the emphasis on goalscoring intent in a *catenaccio* system which he insisted was designed for counter attacking rather than outright defence, as embodied in one of the slogans he pinned up at the club's training camp ('DEFENCE – LESS THAN 30 GOALS! ATTACK - MORE THAN 100 GOALS!'), his recipe for success too often elevated the securing of the back door and operating the hand brake at the expense of the exhilarating speed, flair and razor-sharpness in front of goal which his team proved it was capable of. Little wonder that such bombastic statements alienated many in football, not least Jock Stein, who described them as unnecessary since they detracted from the quality of Herrera's teams, whose achievements spoke for themselves.

Jock Stein could be just as blunt and disciplinarian, a man whom *France Football* described in 1967 as having an iron fist in a velvet glove. Willie Waddell credited Stein with bringing to the club "a sheer efficiency that amazes", highlighting an attention to detail when it came to players: "He jokes with them, he baits them, he drives them, he kids them... but there is method in every action. Everything is done for a purpose – all for the benefit of Celtic Football Club." Stein himself stated that he had his players trained to "thinking the game" and they could now work out things for themselves to a greater degree, a claim he made in a profile by 'A Scottish Football Correspondent' in *The Times* (May 26th 1967) which was a touch adulatory, but not unreservedly so: "As a player he was a lean and thoughtful. Now he is bulky and pleasantly argumentative. He is liked and feared by his players. To them he is a fox and the ultimate authority on all football matters. He plans deeply without submerging individual talents and he is intolerant of deviationists... The stimulating atmosphere and the purposeful training has made new men of them all."

Not everyone would agree about his handling of players. In recent years former Celtic players such as John Fallon, Charlie Gallagher and John Hughes have testified to rude, bullying, ruthless and manipulative traits on the part of a manager whose frightening temper when roused was also part of his Jekyll and Hyde (or at least many-sided) relationship with his players, a degree of edginess created most notably by his barbed wit on the one hand, boisterousness, joviality, wise cracking, and a caring side - largely kept private - on the other. John ('Dixie') Deans, a prolific striker of the early 1970s recalled that Stein "had the ability to shrink you with a torrent of abuse and the next minute make you feel ten feet tall", adding that when he dropped you he didn't tell you why and you were not expected to ask, "you just knew you had it coming." The manager rarely dished out praise, believing it made players susceptible to complacency or big-headedness: if a player wasn't performing to the requisite standard, he had to be told, since otherwise he would think that he was playing well. Stein, never the type to court popularity, appears to have operated a system of what could be described as creative tension geared to maximize the inner self-belief that characterises winners. Billy McNeill has suggested that the manager "orchestrated barneys to get matters off his chest", a theory which gives substance to the rumour that, if Stein had to make a point forcefully to his players at half-time, he would slap his face repeatedly to redden it as much as possible before he entered the dressing room, in order to give the impression that he was angry about their performance. There does seem to be a touch of theatricality about the cunning employed by Stein, who once told his protégé,

Sir Alex Ferguson, that the secret of being an effective manager is "to keep the six players who hate you away from the five that are undecided."

That sounds like a bleak assessment of human nature, but it would be one which fails to take account of the brutal truth that dressing rooms in professional sport are by their nature highly competitive environments, certainly no place for shrinking violets, and there was no shortage of strong and opinionated personalities in those Celtic dressing rooms of the late 1960s and early 1970s. More to the point, it takes no account of the self-imposed strains that characterized Stein's all-encompassing involvement in football. And certainly it did not seem to impact on the pitch, judging by Billy McNeill's repeated insistence that the manager turned Celtic into a formidable, battling playing unit and it was a case of "all for one and one for all" once the players took the field to give expression to their manager's demands for winning, attractive football which lived up to the highest standards of the game as it should be played and which validated his insistence on the values of team-work. He told Bryan Cooney in an article in the *Sunday Herald* in October 2004 that "sometimes he [Stein] was not always easy to love in the traditional sense of the word... He was hard and demanding, but those demands paid off. He gave us dreams we would never have had without him." Even John Hughes, no fan of Stein as we have already seen, has acknowledged Stein's organisational prowess, albeit in a double-edged statement: "What Jock did so well was organize us and get the best out of all the players. He wouldn't give you two bob and would always verbally put down anyone he thought was getting above himself. But he got the results. And when you are at a club like Celtic, you can't live without them" (*Sunday Post*, May 15th 2016). Tommy Gemmell, whose relationship with the manager was turbulent, to say the least, was quoted in September 2016 as saying that "Stein was great for the club, changed everything, made everything possible."

Stein, as football journalist John Blair once asserted in the late 1960s, "lives for Celtic, make no mistake." Celtic, after all, was the club that had dragged him out of obscurity, giving him and his family a degree of security such as he had not known in his life as a part-time footballer and a miner (he had also seen the pits take a terrible toll on his father's health). Celtic was a club which he believed represented the game's finest values, particularly those of loyalty and team spirit. The manager was wont to recall a lesson he had learned from his days as a miner, namely that the danger of individuality degenerating into self-indulgence could be deadly. The men he worked beside, below ground, he recalled, "didn't just get their own work done and walk away, they stayed behind until everyone had completed their task and all was cleared up." Bertie Auld has insisted that Jock Stein's communication with his players was not unilateral, stating that the manager had had an obsession with getting players more deeply involved in the game ever since he (Auld) had been a member of the reserve team that Stein had coached in the late 1950s, and the process continued after Bertie returned to Celtic Park from Birmingham City in 1965: "Four of us would maybe be sitting enjoying a game of solo and he would come over and watch for a while and then ask: 'Remember when we were building up on the right and it broke down? Do you think we might have done such and such?'. Tam Gemmell or one of the others would say: 'That's right, we might have done this or that' and he [Stein] would go away and leave us with the solo game destroyed. Then we would see him sitting with Jimmy Johnstone and Bobby Lennox and the same would go on there. It was only in my latter days at Celtic Park that I twigged what he was at. I realised that he got us thinking and talking about the game and making suggestions, which he accepted with enthusiasm but *he* had put the thoughts into our head. We were only giving them back, but we felt good because we thought they were ours" (as told to John Rafferty of *The Observer*, August 4th 1974).

That unceasing quest for perfection was only one of the reasons, apart from his uncanny, priceless ability to convince players that they were better than they thought they were, which caused some observers, notably Hugh McIlvanney, to believe he was the most comprehensibly equipped manager in the business at a time when formidable personalities such as Bill Shankly and Mark Busby were also operating. It was a talent summed up in an article by Joachim Pfitzner of the East German newspaper *Neues Deutschland*: "You have to be able to enthuse the players for their own sake and for the cause. They have to believe that they are the best players in the world" (June 19th 1967). But one wonders at what cost to family life and health was his obsession with the game. Stein himself was revealing on the matter: "I don't believe those people who say that when they lock the office door they leave their worries behind. If that is the case, I'd give a lot to know how they do it." In an interview for Radio Scotland in the summer of 2015, Hugh McIlvanney revealed that Jock Stein was prone to "a depth of melancholy", the so-called 'black dog', without expanding on the topic. The outwardly confident projection which was enhanced by his build, six feet tall and broader in the shoulders than a blacksmith, may well have concealed a degree of insecurity that perhaps marked him out from cold-blooded technicians such as Helenio Herrera. Football was never far away from his thoughts, his only hobby the odd game of bowls, and he always appeared a restless figure. During that limbo period in 1978 between the ending of his time at Celtic and his brief stint at Leeds United he fretted to his friend Lawrie McMenemy, the Southampton manager, about being without a job in football for the first time in his life and not knowing what to do with himself. His assistant at Celtic Park, Sean Fallon, revealed that "Jock was never happy, he was always looking for 100%... he used to chew stones that he threw into his mouth in the dug-out to relieve the stress" (*Evening Times*, December 31st 1999). It was noticeable too how uncomfortable he could often appear in public. On the day after his greatest triumph, he suddenly cut short a seemingly relaxed interview at the Palácio Hotel to let out a roar after Jimmy Johnstone's poolside antics caught his attention: "Cut it out, Jimmy, you'll get hurt!" The startled journalist looked on this incident with a mixture of awe and wonderment: "He had an ear for me, but an eye for his players at the same time." On another occasion, asked by a photographer to "Give me a smile, Jock", the manager snapped back "I *am* smiling." Given this self-imposed pressure, one can only guess at the human cost of the sheer force of will and commitment that it took for this complex figure to turn around the moribund club that was Celtic so quickly and dramatically and lead it to sustained success for a decade. Football perhaps became too much of an endless, fatal obsession for him, in contrast to Helenio Herrera, whose death in Venice in 1997, when in his 80s and in retirement, is marked by a gravestone urn in the shape of the European Cup. The Jock Stein story ended in September 1985 at the age of 62 after he forsook his medication in order to concentrate, as manager of Scotland, on a crucial World Cup match against Wales. That endless quest for perfection, that fear of failure, had, surely, exerted a terrible toll.

CHAPTER 6
A Time of Reckoning

The defeat in Turin on May 7th was perhaps the defining moment of Inter's season. No longer were they being seen as champions-elect, as *Gazzetta dello Sport* had hailed them with four games remaining. With his captain Armando Picchi now suggesting that a title triumph had probably been taken for granted ("the celebrations had started too early", he observed cryptically), Herrera acknowledged, after weeks of denial, that he was worried about the quality and depth of his squad, stating that it contained only fifteen men of first-team standard. The critics pointed to poor recruitment, a notable contributory factor being the coach's failing to see eye-to-eye with Italo Allodi, the club's administrator, responsible for transfers and salary negotiations. The case of one particular signing highlighted Herrera's failure to 'manage' the season, not least in terms of his deficient squad rotation. The Brazilian striker Luis Vinícius de Menezes, better known as Vinicio, the top scorer in Serie 'A' in the 1965-66 season with Lanerossi Vicenza, was seen as a deputy for Sandro Mazzola, but he was barely in the door at the San Siro before Herrera was dismissing him as too slow, mentally and physically. After scoring only once in nine matches in all competitions during season 1966-67 he returned to Vicenza. Yet Herrera remained defiant, expressing his confidence that the season would still end well for Inter despite a home draw with Napoli on May 14th, since Juventus could only themselves draw at Mantova that same day, leaving Inter two points clear at the top. An unprecedented treble – Championship, Coppa Italia and the European Cup - was still on.

A relieved Herrera boarded an early-morning flight to Lisbon the following day. He was there mainly to finalise the team's hotel arrangements for the European Cup final, including a demand for exclusive use of their Muxito base which led to existing guests being moved out, a situation which did not go down well in the local press and added to his team's unpopularity, but he also took the opportunity to fit other matters into his busy schedule. He visited the *Estádio Nacional*, the venue for the final, making a point of praising the quality of the pitch and "reserving" the dressing room of his choice, described by a Portuguese newspaper as "the lucky one"; he called in at the Portuguese Football Federation (FPF) to pick up two balls of the type to be used in the final, one of which was used, at his request, during the league match against Fiorentina the following Sunday, four days before the European Cup final, and, finally, he engaged the services of Dr. Silva Rocha, the masseur/physician of Belenenses (a club once coached by Herrera) and the Portuguese national team, for medical help when Inter's "undoubtedly fatigued and saturated" (in the words of Herrera) players were in Lisbon the following week. The temporary recruitment of Silva Rocha, as the Dutch football magazine *Revu* inferred, may have been a reaction to criticism back home: "Herrera couldn't, or wouldn't, see that his team was struggling, with ever greater pressure being put on Inter's medical team as time was taking its toll on some members of the squad, all the while turning a deaf ear to the supporters' clamour for more entertaining, less functional displays." Before returning to Milan, Herrera told local reporters that Celtic would be "fearsome opponents" but added that Inter's defence would cope with the Scots' pace, and then appeared on local radio and television with a message that sounded more like an instruction rather than an appeal: "Portuguese fans, you must cheer us on against Celtic. I am your friend and we want to keep the European Cup safely in Latin hands." Predictably, that message went down like a lead balloon. Benfica fans were still smarting from Inter's seeming high-handedness and alleged manoeuvering in ensuring that the European Cup final two years earlier was a home match for the Italian club, who duly retained their crown with a 1-0 victory on a rain-sodden San Siro pitch which several observers thought was unplayable.

The growing suspicion that Herrera was guilty of self-deception was reinforced the following weekend by yet another home draw (1-1), this time at the hands of Fiorentina, which reduced Inter's lead at the top to a mere point ahead of Juventus, who won 1-0 at Vicenza that same afternoon of May 21st. It would now be a fight to the death for the title when the challengers played their final matches on June 1st. This was a body blow to Herrera, who admitted that he had hoped to depart for Lisbon with the boost of the championship being more firmly in his grasp. Inter had left the field to the sounds of boos and whistling after struggling to get going against a visiting side whose feeble finishing prevented them from scoring four or five goals, a reflection of Inter's alarming inattentiveness to their recruiting inadequacies. The disarray in their home defence was partly the result of Mario Corso, normally a winger/midfielder, being deployed as a spare defender, a role for which he lacked the grit and speed to perform effectively. A reporter who visited Inter's training camp the following day noted that all the usual bounce had gone from Herrera, "a man alone" amid the complex's palatial facilities. For several weeks, Allan Herron of the *Sunday Mail* had been learning from his Italian contact, Gianni de Felice of the Milan-based *Corriere dello Sport,* of the extent of Herrera's concern about the obstacle that Celtic presented to his ambition for a third Champions' Cup: "Gianni told me that Helenio, normally a rather aloof and arrogant individual, was genuinely worried about the damage that could be inflicted on his defence by the pace of Lennox and Chalmers, not to mention the disruption that could be caused by the elusiveness of Jimmy Johnstone."

Herrera knew that he would have to travel to Lisbon without two of his more celebrated performers, both Suárez and Jaïr having aggravated injuries against Fiorentina which would rule them out eventually from the European Cup final against Celtic. Both before and after that final, Herrera and certain journalists would make much play about their absence in Lisbon, using it as an excuse for Inter's defeat. However, that takes no account of the feeling of some observers who had been covering their matches that Luis Suárez was, as one reporter put it, "playing more on reputation than current reality." One of Inter's favourite ploys was for Mazzola and Cappellini to run out to the left in an attempt to lure defenders out of position, thus enabling Suárez and Corso (often supported by full back Giacinto Facchetti) to make a thrust down the middle, but this tactic would be undermined by Suárez's apparent recent unwillingness to venture forth from his own half of the pitch. Such diffidence was a weakness that had been identified two years earlier by Herrera, no less, when he criticized Suárez for overindulging the passing game at the expense of grafting as Inter wilted in the face of Liverpool's barrage in the European Cup semi-final first leg at Anfield, a forewarning of what he would have had to face in Lisbon, after which at least one journalist concluded that Suárez would not have coped with Celtic's tempo: "The Scots were faster with the ball at their feet than Inter were without it." In his report of the Fiorentina match in the *Scottish Daily Mail* (May 22nd 1967), Ronald Waters highlighted further evidence of the Spaniard's untimely decline in effectiveness, noting that the playmaker appeared to have lost his midfield calm, displaying an inability to find his forwards with his usual accuracy.

Perhaps his displays were being affected by an approach from Real Madrid with a view to joining them when his contract expired on June 30th. The attraction of a huge signing-on fee, lucrative salary and lower taxes in Spain would also have been a temptation for Helenio Herrera, a twin target for Real Madrid. It was well known that Herrera was disillusioned at Inter, believed to be harbouring a feeling that he could do no more at the club he had guided for seven years, and he was not relishing the prospect of a massive re-building job on an ageing squad. As it happened, both Suárez and Herrera opted to remain in Milan, albeit the latter for only one more season, his departure coming in tandem with the long-anticipated retirement of Angelo Moratti from the club's presidency.

As for Jaïr, he had not been a regular during season 1966-67 due to a mixture of injury and loss of form. Herrera was known to be unhappy with the Brazilian's lack of tactical discipline and his unpredictability. Speculation in the Italian sporting press that Jaïr would be shipped out at the end of season became fact when he joined Roma. Herrera's assigning of the blame for Inter's reverse in Lisbon to the absence of the aforementioned duo would come as no surprise to the much-respected Vittorio Pozzo, the correspondent for Turin's *La Stampa* and formerly the manager of Italy's World Cup-winning teams of 1934 and 1938. He told John Mackenzie of the *Scottish Daily Express* in Lisbon that Herrera had never been so worried before about a match and would make his excuses in advance just in case of defeat.

However, for all the perceived woes of the *Nerazzurri*, Douglas Eadie, a Scot apparently resident in Italy, reported a seeming consensus in that country: "That Inter might just lose this year's European Cup Final was not considered" (*The Scotsman*, weekend magazine section, May 20th 1967). Much of that conviction was based on the viewing of Italian TV's live coverage, watched by Herrera and his players, of Celtic's home semi-final leg against Dukla Prague which had given the impression that the Scots were possessed more of physical force than the technical range and command deemed necessary to compete successfully with Inter. The commentator repeatedly said during the transmission that Inter were far superior to Celtic, an assertion backed up by Dezso Solti (a Hungarian employed by Inter as an "observer", though the sports writer Brian Glanville would later allege that Solti was also used in a far more sinister role, that of a match-fixer). Whatever, with the Scottish club having been identified early on by Herrera as a threat to his European aspirations, Solti was spotted at Celtic's European matches that season, taking notes and compiling diagrams and dossiers. After his watching brief at that Celtic vs. Dukla match, he dismissed Celtic's chances of winning the competition, his quote in French magazine *Miroir du Football* delivering a withering assessment: "Inter would perhaps have problems to resolve in front of a Glasgow crowd, but not on neutral territory, for the two teams which we saw at Parkhead do not have sufficient class to feature in the semi-finals. Their presence there seems accidental." Eadie begged to differ with that conclusion. Having watched Inter several times recently, he pronounced his verdict that they were a team of "football dandies" who earned an "ethereal respect" from teams acquainted with a more exalted level of football, but against teams with everything to gain [e.g. Celtic] they were "strangely negative." Expanding on his theory, Eadie said that "If you don't believe in ghosts and certainly McNeill and Gemmell, Murdoch and Auld don't, you'll treat them as flesh and blood, and that's where, often literally, the Inter players fall down. From what I know of both teams, Celtic are precisely the kind of side to beat Inter. Theirs is the direct, forcing play against which Inter are at their finicky poorest."

Significantly, and encouragingly so for Celtic, Inter had only emerged victorious from their ties against British sides (Everton, Rangers and Liverpool) by the narrowest of margins. Indeed two years earlier at Ibrox Park, Rangers had inflicted on Inter their very first defeat in the European Cup. Frank Arrighi, a Glasgow-born Inter fan who has watched his favourites home and abroad for several decades and acted as Inter's interpreter for their European Cup match against Celtic at Parkhead in 1972, recalls that it was so cold in Glasgow on match night in 1965 that an employee of the club's city centre hotel was sent out to buy gloves for players who nevertheless still looked distinctly uncomfortable on the Ibrox Park pitch that evening. Arrighi, who had not regarded Celtic at the outset as potential winners of the competition, agrees with Eadie that Inter lacked the *grinta* (Italian for 'fighting spirit, determination') of Celtic which the former began to fear after the Scots had underlined their threat with a last-gasp quarter-final elimination of Vojvodina. Wet, icy conditions of all types, regarded as traditional allies of British clubs, would certainly not be a problem for Herrera in Portugal, but, for all his disdain for the British style of play, the Inter coach would not be relishing the prospect of facing resolute, stubborn opponents from the hard-nosed city of Glasgow.

CHAPTER 7
On the Eve

Celtic wrapped up their domestic programme with a 2-0 home League victory over Kilmarnock on Monday evening 15th May, thus winning the title by a three-point margin, before heading the following morning to Seamill on the Ayrshire coast, for over half a century the club's favourite base for preparation and relaxation. It was, for Stein, both a means of keeping the squad ticking over during the countdown to Lisbon and an opportunity – by means of showing a film of the celebrated 1960 Real Madrid vs. Eintracht Frankfurt final – of underlining the standards to which his players should aspire and instilling in them a sense of occasion. His attention to detail was such that, by the time they left Glasgow a few days later, every Celtic player was made aware of how they would dress, the necessity of punctuality for meals and transport, and how they should conduct themselves. Celtic's image was paramount. Nothing was left to chance. Archie Macpherson told Pat Woods in a recent interview that "Stein scrutinised *every* aspect of preparation that might impact on the final."

It was, then, a supremely refreshed, fit and expectant squad which returned to Glasgow in time for a weekend with family and loved ones before reporting to Celtic Park on Monday 22nd May for a final training session before departure for Lisbon, and a thorough briefing on Inter's tactics, strengths and weaknesses which was conducted by the manager in a manner which indicated his belief (indeed near certainty) that his players would win if his plans to unsettle their opponents were carried out – "You'll beat Inter because you are better and stronger."

Meanwhile, Herrera felt the need for a morale booster for his squad after the setback against Fiorentina. At the training camp after their final session prior to departure for Lisbon the following day, he called together the players and backroom staff to toast the "the future fortunes" of the club with a glass of champagne. The reports were of an upbeat coach who spoke to the press afterwards as follows: "I have always said that great teams and real men come to the fore in difficult situations. It is easy to be champions when all is going well. I'm sure the real Inter will be on show in Lisbon."

Spirits were high the following morning when Celtic players, backroom staff, officials and guests gathered at Celtic Park before boarding the bus to Glasgow Airport, with Bertie Auld adding to the sense of ease and anticipation by brandishing a 'best wishes' telegram purportedly sent from Buckingham Palace. Jock Stein set the tone for the trip after the De Havilland Comet 4 chartered from Dan Air took to the skies, taking off his jacket before strolling up and down the plane and joking with his fellow passengers. However, Celtic soon got down to business shortly after touching down at Lisbon's Portela airport, where that day a flight from Switzerland also arrived, one with a precious cargo stowed in its hold. After being on display the previous week in the window of Stadelmann's, the jewellers/goldsmiths in Berne, the new European Cup, placed in a large blue box with gold handles, would now await its first winning captain.

The twenty-strong Celtic squad had barely checked into their headquarters, the Hotel Palácio in Estoril, before the players were bused to a training session at a ground adjacent to the *Estádio Nacional* (National Stadium), the venue for the final. It was a training pitch Stein was familiar with, his Dunfermline side having used it prior to losing an Inter City Fairs Cup play-off to the holders, Valencia, at the Restelo stadium (the home of Belenenses) four years earlier. The opportunity was taken afterwards to have a look at the National Stadium itself, the players expressing their delight at a surface on which "they could have staged a bowls match." By now the players knew who would represent the club in the most prestigious match of its long history, meaning that there was no place for John Fallon (albeit he was the reserve goalkeeper should Ronnie Simpson be injured during the final), Ian Young, John Cushley, Jim Brogan, Willie O'Neill, Charlie Gallagher, David Cattanach, John Hughes and Joe McBride (the latter two both being injured). It was, indeed, Celtic's good fortune to have such an impressive pool of players, the bedrock of the club's success in the Stein years. When one considers that Celtic had started that season with 32 players on their books, including the up-and-coming David Hay and Lou Macari, there is a fair case to be made for the belief that the club could have fielded two quality sides; this was, of course, in contrast to the increasingly limited playing resources available to Inter, as indicated in the previous chapter.

Prior to the final, the emphasis was on relaxation. The players were superbly conditioned and thus there was no need for high-intensity training. "Jock was more interested in resting us than putting us through our paces", says Steve

Chalmers, "We simply carried out loosening-up exercises." As a result of Stein learning that Manchester United, three goals up from their European Cup-Winners' Cup quarter-final first leg against Sporting Lisbon three years earlier, had (allegedly) lazed around in the sun and exited from the competition, and recalling that Jimmy Johnstone had been badly affected by over-exposure to the sun in Bermuda, the first leg of the 1966 close season tour of North America, the manager's only real stricture was that his players be aware of such a danger.

The setting provided Stein himself with the ideal opportunity to hold court with the media poolside and project Celtic's image. Overall, the build-up was designed to relieve the pressure in the last days and hours before the match, and the club's base proved to be an inspired choice in that regard. It had long been seen as the most glamorous hotel on a coast which had long been home to Europe's exile aristocracy – among them King Umberto II of Italy, the last sovereign of that country and a guest of honour at the final itself – and, during the Second World War, a major focal point in an area of officially neutral Portugal known as the "crossroads of espionage", where Allied and Axis agents warily circled each other as they kept an eye on shipping and aerial movements in that part of the Atlantic. One of those operators, involved in naval intelligence, was Ian Fleming, soon to become famous as the author of the James Bond books, at least one of which (*Casino Royale*) reflected the prevalent shadowy goings-on (and it is interesting to note that the original film version of the novel was shot at this hotel).

As it turned out, Inter were not so fortunate in the choice of their base, Muxito in the Vale dos Gatos (The Valley of the Cats) on the south side of the Tagus estuary, a fair distance from Lisbon. George Aitken of Glasgow's *Evening Citizen* was distinctly unimpressed when he paid a visit to their luxurious, but isolated headquarters: "The buildings were screened by trees and to reach the Italian team's headquarters you have to swing off the main road and take to the country track. The players were located in two-man bungalows and an Italian flag flies above the central box of houses. Herrera is playing a hard-to-get Garbo role. It doesn't look like an act. He seems genuinely concerned – even worried – about the outcome of tomorrow's game. He is brusque in his contact with the press. He so clearly wants to be alone with his players." Several accounts have suggested that the feeling appears to have been less than reciprocal on the part of a squad who had been tiring of their coach's dictatorial approach and now paid greater heed to the views of their influential captain, Armando Picchi, who had been striving to soften the hard edge of Herrera's strict regime, albeit unsuccessfully. Such was the sense of alienation resulting from Herrera's refusal to listen that defender Tarcisio Burgnich would complain years later that the prison-like seclusion of their Muxito hotel was so stressful that he was kept awake at night by the sound of team-mates vomiting.

Herrera was either guilty of turning a blind eye to situations or pulling the wool over the eyes of his critics in the face of all the evidence that *La Grande Inter* was crumbling. How else to account for his insistence that "the Portuguese public is behind us" and his dismissal of all talk of tiredness in his squad, swatting it aside with a prediction that "the character, strength and spirit" of his players would ensure that the next two matches would bring them the European Cup in Lisbon and the domestic championship at Mantova? The suspicion that he was whistling in the dark was reinforced when the finalists held a training session at the *Estádio Nacional* on the morning of 24th May, the day before the final. Tommy Gallacher, a son of Patsy of Celtic fame, a fine player in his own right with Queens Park and Dundee but now turned journalist with a Dundee paper, thought that the Inter players looked "highly strung" during their rigidly structured and intense training session, at the end of which Herrera told the assembled international press that Celtic was a very fit team which had plenty of spirit but was inclined to be rather impetuous and clearly not in Inter's class, underscoring his dismissal of the Glasgow side by saying "Of course Inter Milan will win" as he sauntered off the pitch after the questioning had finished.

Now it was Celtic's turn and they had arrived, in contrast to the stony silence afforded to Inter by the watching crowd, to a mixture of Celtic fans and intrigued Portuguese chanting "Cel-tic, Cel-tic, Cel-tic", a clear rebuttal of Herrera's assessment of the balance of local support. Initially, Herrera indicated that Inter would not be staying behind to watch Celtic's preparations, but five minutes later he changed his mind and his players, still dressed in their tracksuits, were ordered to sit in the temporary, specially constructed press stand to watch a comparatively brief Celtic training session which Sandro Mazzola believes to this day was "Inter's greatest mistake", causing the Italian side to underestimate the Scots. Nearly half a century later, he recalled in *La Gazzetta dello Sport* that the Inter players had looked on "goggle-eyed, laughing up their sleeves" before returning to their hotel, thinking that "they could make a meal of these mad Scotsmen" after they had watched a light work-out followed by a practice match that he claimed (wrongly) had involved journalists and hangers-on. It was, he said, a sort of fairground atmosphere: "Total confusion – we couldn't work out what was going on, who was who, who was even a player. It was hard to create the right level of worry or anxiety."

Mazzola, like his team-mates (including Armando Picchi and Giacinto Facchetti) sharing note-taking with Herrera on the latter's instruction, had been duped by the cunning Stein, who ordered his players to do some sprints, pass the ball about and have a practice match, the latter a light-hearted kickabout during which they were encouraged to indulge in banter and mickey-taking as they also swapped roles, with goalkeeper Ronnie Simpson, for example, playing as an attacker. Stein had instructed his players to "show nothing", and thus it was to be just as much an exercise in futility for the Italian onlookers as it had been during an earlier round in Switzerland for the FC Zurich officials who, notebooks in hand, had recorded details of a similar session when Bobby Lennox, endowed with electric pace, was ordered to canter around the pitch and Tommy Gemmell deployed to take on the goalkeeper role. After the training session, a bullish Stein gave the impression of a man firmly in control of the situation, whilst at the same time wasting no opportunity to get his points across to the encircling press corps, pouring scorn on Herrera's tendency to harp on about the absence of Suárez and Jaïr and emphasising Celtic's determination to attack and entertain. "We have no problems, everything is fine. If we lose, we will have no excuses. Believe me, there's no problem whether Suárez plays or not. Bicicli is playing? Fine, he's a part of the Inter squad. For me, a real team is made up of fifteen, sixteen or seventeen men. Do you think we at Celtic haven't had our problems? We lost our top goal scorer, centre-forward Joe McBride, with a torn cartilage. Isn't that a severe occurrence?" It had not gone un-noticed that throughout the training sessions, the rival coaches had kept their distance from one another.

That morning the Celtic manager had assured readers of *A Bola* that spectators at the final "would be getting good value for their money", and John Rafferty of *The Scotsman*, reporting on the applause of local observers during the training session at an adjacent pitch the previous evening, quoted Stein as saying "It's up to us to see to it that we deserve their support by playing well." He left the *Estádio Nacional* delighted by further evidence that the local fans were swinging towards Celtic and by news of the green and white hordes pouring into Lisbon. Three years earlier Celtic supporters had been denied a trip abroad, to Brussels, for the European Cup-winners' Cup final by a sensational semi-final return leg collapse (0-4, aggregate 3-4) in Budapest at the hands of M.T.K., a shattering blow to the fans who, according to *The Celtic F.C. Supporters' Association Handbook 1964/65*, had begun "to look for that extra Sunday shift at work, to severely curtail the weekend spending and to conjure up how to scrape the few pounds together to take them to the final, while quotations were being sought from travel agencies and airline companies." Now they were on the banks of the Tagus in force, a boost for morale which gave an extra edge to Stein's assertion that the advantage had moved to the Scots: "Inter are now more worried about us: we will play an offensive game – we've come to play a game of football, not to fight a war." More importantly, he clearly sensed that his men were ready, physically and mentally, to overcome – or at least challenge – the Continental perception of British football as unimaginative, over-physical, predictable, tactically naïve and technically backward, with the players lacking in initiative, mere slaves to an outmoded style of play.

Those critics could point to repeated failure by the 'Anglo-Saxons' - as the Continent tended to dub British sides - at the highest level of European competition (i.e. the European Cup) to circumvent defence in depth when practiced by visiting teams, an inability to defend in depth when abroad, and a lack of subtlety when attempting to overcome teams of the class of Benfica, Real Madrid and the Milanese giants. Meeting the champion Continental sides could be a humiliating and distressing experience. Hugh Taylor of the *Daily Record* described Rangers' 0-6 defeat by Real Madrid at the Bernabeu Stadium in October 1963 as "men playing against boys - little boys in blue… little boys lost in a maze of soccer magic they could never equal, beaten by moves they'd never even dreamed of, never mind experienced and tried out." Jean-Philippe Rethacker of *L'Equipe* hinted that Liverpool were guilty of over-confidence, "as if a space was already being made in the trophy room for the Cup" following their 1965 semi-final first leg shredding of Inter Milan at Anfield which was overturned to the Italians' advantage in the San Siro. After Manchester United were ousted at the semi-final stage in 1966 by Partizan Belgrade they were labeled by a French magazine as "a team which relied solely on the inspiration of individuals." Their distraught manager, Matt Busby, made no secret of his belief that his club had blown his best ever chance of conquering Europe and was at the point of resigning until, as he revealed to Scottish journalist Gerry McNee two decades later, he watched from his car - shortly after that mortifying exit - as a party of blind people crossed a road near Old Trafford, causing him to reflect that there were more important things in life than football.

It was now up to Jock Stein's men to bridge the gap between aspiration and achievement, to rid Britain of the 'bystanders' image which had bedeviled its clubs since the inception of the competition. Intriguingly, one noted Scottish football personality had insisted on STV's *Scotsport* programme that such a feat was not beyond top native clubs: Jim Baxter, of Rangers and Scotland fame no less, said this in the early 60s, doubtless believing that his club, then the strongest and richest in the country, had the best chance of success. Clearly, he was not thinking of his club's fiercest rivals, Celtic, a team which he once admitted to holding in little regard during his first spell at Ibrox (1960-65), saying "I honestly never felt they were likely to beat us."

Now it was Celtic's turn to joust with a representative of the European elite. Happily, Celtic could count on the backing of around 10-15,000 fans, who were massing in Lisbon after having travelled by plane, train, bus, car and on foot. (The extent of hitchhiking has been greatly underestimated: one fan, John McCarroll from Croy, spent twelve days on the road thumbing lifts.) Inevitably, there were problems on the way - delays caused by unfamiliarity with Continental road signs being one – but at least one busload had a slice of luck when a 'Good Samaritan' came to their aid. A few days after the final the *Sunday Post* reported that the minister of the Church of Scotland in Lisbon, the Reverend Kenneth Tyson, put up fifty-two supporters from the Shotts, Hamilton and Bellshill area in the gardens (mainly) of his manse, fortunately in favourable weather. Their bus had broken down in Madrid as the result of engine trouble, but they had managed to get on to a flight to Lisbon, the added expense apparently leaving a lot of the fans out pocket. One of them had recalled reading the Reverend Tyson's offer of assistance to fans in a previous edition of the newspaper and had kept a copy of the article. The report added that the Good Samaritan had even gone to the lengths of tracking down the bus, which was repaired and refuelled before being driven to the Portuguese capital for the fans' journey home, and the minister himself was quoted in the *Sunday Post* a few days after the Final as saying "They were a great bunch. In fact, so were all the Celtic fans in Lisbon. You can tell the folks at home, the Scots are welcome back, any time. Celtic did Scotland proud, and so did the fans."

Donald Bruce, in his dispatch to the *Daily Record* on the night of Wednesday 24th May, captured the scene as the Celtic legions anticipated what they believed was the club's date with destiny: "Lisbon, sweltering city of a million twinkling lights under a pale yellow moon, belongs tonight to Glasgow. They came in their thousands, the Celtic fans to take over the city for tomorrow's European Cup Final with Inter Milan at Lisbon's National Stadium. Frankly, Lisbon, which has seen many sights, has never seen anything like this before." Well, give or take the Great Lisbon earthquake of 1755... It was, perhaps, a pardonable exaggeration from a reporter caught up in the infectious atmosphere prevailing in the city, highlighted by the news that a planeload of fans had left Dublin armed with good luck shillelaghs courtesy of Aer Lingus. Given Celtic's origins, it somehow seemed appropriate that the famed luck of the Irish was being drafted in to the cause. However, one group was an exception to all the hysteria, namely a bedraggled and weary bunch seen easing themselves out of their cramped cars in the Avenida da Liberdade around 10 p.m. that evening, after leaving Glasgow 86 hours earlier for a 1,750 miles drive. Most of them indicated that they were heading on to the beaches at Estoril and Cascais to sleep out, a reminder of the tight budgets on which thousands of the Celtic fans were operating. Time to dream of the morrow.

CHAPTER 8
A Special Correspondent

Celtic's popularity was evident within hours of their setting foot in Lisbon. When the players arrived for a training session at "a rustic ground" adjacent to the *Estádio Nacional*, they were accorded, said John Mackenzie of the *Scottish Daily Express*, "a fantastic reception from a huge crowd of schoolboys who formed an avenue and cheered the Celtic players from their bus with chants of 'Celtic... Celtic', beaming a welcome as they clapped." The chances are that this new-found fan club stemmed from the public relations work of an 'actor' in the drama of Lisbon whose role has never been previously recognised in Scotland, and yet, despite his self-deprecatory stance on the matter in an interview with co-author David Frier, he made a significant contribution to promoting Celtic in his native land ahead of the final. He is a Portuguese citizen, now in his seventies: today he enjoys a pleasant retirement in Belgium, and he may seem an unlikely secret agent in the clash between Herrera's Inter and Jock Stein's Celtic, but in truth without his advance work the Glasgow club might as well have come from the moon for all the people of Lisbon knew about it, particularly its players. After all, Portugal's only previous experience of Celtic, a towsy Fairs Cities Cup tie with Leixões in the autumn of 1964 in which three players (including Chalmers and Young of Celtic) were sent off at the *Estádio do Mar*, had left (at best) a mixed impression of the Scots, at least as reflected in Portuguese press reports, one of which characterised the encounter as "vulgar fairground football." So forgettable was this tie that, less than three years after it took place, one Lisbon newspaper's coverage of the European Cup final stated that it was Celtic's first appearance in the country, an error that was, however, soon corrected.

The role of Miguel de Paiva Couceiro in the Lisbon story is partly simply a stroke of good fortune, due to his period as a student at Strathclyde University, Glasgow, from the autumn of 1965 to the summer of 1967. The timing, both for Miguel and for Celtic, could not have been better, but if it had not been for the warmth of the reception which he found in Scotland in the mid-1960s and the fresh, exciting football being played by Celtic at the time, then he probably would not have had the enthusiasm or inspiration to play the role behind the scenes which he did in Celtic's greatest victory. Of course, international student mobility in the 1960s was much more restricted than it is now, and no doubt Miguel benefitted to some degree from his family background: the Paiva Couceiros are a distinguished family from the Portuguese aristocracy, with some of his ancestors playing a significant role in national political and military history as far back as the 1830s, and with other members of his family being close confidants of King Carlos in the early years of the twentieth century. So it is no surprise that the family has a long history of connections with the rest of Europe and the wider world (amongst other things, his nephew retains the title of Count of Paraty in Brazil, an honour ceded to the family by the Portuguese Crown in 1813). Miguel himself points out that he came to Strathclyde University because he needed to obtain a degree in Applied Chemistry from an English-speaking university in order to go and work in his father's sugar production plant in Mozambique (which, at the time, was still considered part of Portugal, but where exportation to some of the English-speaking countries surrounding it would have been a vital part of the growth plans for the business). There was also a vague family connection with Britain, as Miguel points out his own (distant) ancestry: "My paternal great-grandmother was called Helena Armstrong Mitchell; unfortunately, we haven't been able to find out a lot about her ancestry, but I believe that she was from the north of England, near Newcastle, very near Scotland, where she had had to flee because she was a Protestant (from Ireland)." One further interesting family connection is with one of the most famous buildings in Portugal, the Mateus palace, near Vila Real in northern Portugal, famous as a prominent feature on the labels of Mateus Rosé wine bottles: "My great-grandmother [Dona Isabel de] Sousa Botelho was born in that palace; she was the mother-in-law of Henrique de Paiva Couceiro." Henrique was Miguel's paternal grandfather and Governor of Portuguese Angola for two years in the first half of the twentieth century, while his father, also called Miguel, was a Governor of Diu, in India, who was noted for his significant efforts to improve the standard of living within the province, before he moved to South Africa and then Mozambique in 1953 and set up the sugar processing plant in which Miguel was due to take up employment.

Miguel was no mean sportsman himself. He was a member of the successful Sporting Lisbon roller hockey squad which won the 1964 Portuguese Championship in that sport, and as a youth he was also on the books of their football team, being coached by notable figures in the club's history such as the Argentine Mário Imbelloni, José Travassos and Juca, before then spending a brief period with the youth section at then second-division Estoril Praia (who were promoted to the Portuguese first division in 2012), based in the exclusive coastal resort where the Celtic party were housed in May 1967. Indeed, his sporting career might have continued in Scotland, as he was given a trial as a goalkeeper with Greenock Juniors in the autumn of 1965 (with a photo feature on him in the *Evening Citizen* of December 19th 1965), but, as Miguel recalls these events himself, a combination of bad winter weather, the distance involved in commuting between his accommodation in Glasgow and Greenock and his commitments at the University led him to give up pursuing this career any further at the time.

Given this background, it is not surprising that he should have taken an interest in sport while he was in Glasgow. Since Celtic wore shirts essentially identical to those of his own favoured Lisbon team, and with the initiative in Scottish football having clearly passed to the east end of the city by the end of season 1965-66, Miguel became a regular attender at Celtic matches. That he should have been in Scotland during the club's greatest ever season was a matter of luck, for as Celtic's profile in Europe rose, it was not long before the young man was engaged by Portugal's principal sports newspaper, *A Bola*, to act as their correspondent in Glasgow. The edition of the *Celtic View* published in the week before the final a letter in which he, "a fanatical Celtic supporter", informed the club's supporters that he had written some 5,300 words in total about the team for *A Bola*, and he expressed his certainty that "Portuguese readers who read them will become Celtic supporters before they make their way to watch them at the National Stadium." He went on to thank the club's players and management for making themselves available to him, as well as two or three other named individuals, including James E. Handley (the Marist known as Brother Clare), the author of *The Celtic Story*, for inducting him in all matters Celtic, and he closed his letter by observing that "since the European Cup can't stay in Lisbon, there is only one place it can go – Parkhead!"

In fact, Paiva Couceiro rather underplays his own contribution here. His closest friend in Glasgow at the time (and now), Denis Lavery (who is now a senior figure in the Celtic Charity Foundation and who travelled to Lisbon for the final) expressed no doubts at all as to Miguel's contribution to Celtic's success in the European Cup final, informing co-author David Frier that he had "no doubt that *A Bola* certainly influenced Portuguese supporters" when they read his articles. There is also a moment in the official *History of Celtic Football Club* DVD, issued by the club in 2008, where an energetic and enthusiastic Lisbon local shows the edition of *A Bola* published on the day of the match to a group of interested Celtic supporters in the city centre (and no doubt that same scene was repeated elsewhere in the city that day). As a result of his extensive research on the final, co-author Pat Woods can vouch for the fact that the newspaper's coverage of the event was second to none.

Clearly, the extensive coverage of Celtic in the newspaper over several weeks had had its effect: Miguel's contributions included a short, but revealing interview with Jock Stein on May 13th 1967; a very thorough report on the match in which Celtic had clinched the League title at Ibrox earlier in the month, in the edition of May 20th; interviews with Tommy Gemmell, Ronnie Simpson, Billy McNeill and Jimmy Johnstone in the same edition; and profiles of individual players. For example, Tommy Gemmell is described in the paper on May 11th as the best defender in Britain – and remember that this would have placed him above recognised international stars such as Bobby Moore, the captain in England's World Cup triumph in 1966. The interview with Stein reveals another demonstration of the Celtic manager's gift for placing the right idea in people's minds at the right time, striking a chord with the Portuguese by warm, sincere praise for their own footballing hero, Eusébio, and whetting their appetite for the final by describing his own team as playing 'the football of the future' (May 13th). In the May 18th edition, veteran goalkeeper Ronnie Simpson calmly, but pointedly and confidently, states that "I am already used to winning in Lisbon", a reference to Hibernian's 3-1 Fairs Cities' Cup victory over Belenenses in September 1961, when he also took the opportunity to visit the *Estádio Nacional*, which he described as "the most beautiful stadium I have ever seen." It was also an edition in which chairman Bob Kelly stated his and the club's wish that the final be seen as a stage for Celtic to be seen as "*the* promoters of attacking football", while captain Billy McNeill said that the team wanted to win over the crowd by their positive approach, focusing his attention on the supporters of Sporting Lisbon, a club which also played in green and white hoops. One further item to note is the reporting of comments attributed to Helenio Herrera (and, to the best of our knowledge, never reported in the Scottish press) after his spying visit to Glasgow in early May, which should dispel any notion that he at least was unaware of the quality of the opposition which he was to face in Lisbon: "Celtic for me were like a new world to discover. If I didn't know about them, then Inter could lose the Lisbon final in the first five minutes. In spite of everything, I do not dare say that we are going to win this final [a stance he changed on the eve of the final]. I repeat that Celtic are extraordinarily strong. It would be a very serious error to underestimate their strength" (published in *A Bola*, May 11th 1967).

So, these articles clearly did much to create an expectation about Celtic in advance of their journey to Lisbon, but there was an element of chance in how all of this came about. Miguel's own explanation is as follows: "In my first year in Glasgow, I knew another student from my home town of Oeiras, João Lacasta, who was studying Naval Engineering. He also knew the Lavery family, who were keen Celtic fans (being from an Irish background), and he introduced me to the family, who were two brothers and two sisters, and his father, who went with us to the football. In my first year in Glasgow I think I didn't go to the football, and I don't remember João having gone to matches, but once João left Scotland my friendship with Denis (Lavery) and his brother Jimmy grew, and we went every Saturday – in those days the games were played on Saturdays, and on Saturday afternoons we would go all four, Lavery senior, the two sons and me. It was natural that I should lean towards Celtic in view of them having similar green-and-white hoops to Sporting and since they were Catholics. I slowly learned not to like the Rangers very much, who were their great rivals. Eventually I became a regular at Parkhead, and I also went to many away games. My enthusiasm grew, and I became a fanatical Celtic supporter. It was the golden year for Celtic, in 1966-67; by the time that Celtic qualified for the European Cup final, and the Scottish Cup Final was also around that time, I was also more involved with Celtic and with the players."

However, these words in themselves only tell a part of the story. Amongst Miguel's most prized memories from his close connection with Celtic relate to his assignment from *A Bola* to get the Celtic viewpoint on their upcoming European Cup clashes with Benfica in the autumn of 1969. It is a series of photographs of him, taken in the Celtic dressing room at Hampden Park in the immediate aftermath of the 1969-70 League Cup final against St. Johnstone (in one he is seen holding one handle of the trophy, alongside Jimmy McGrory, while others show him conversing at ease with Jock Stein, Billy McNeill and Steve Chalmers). Not every foreign football enthusiast who passes through Glasgow achieves this type of access to Celtic legends!

Again, Miguel takes up the story: "For some reason I always seem to have had the ability or good luck to open doors without really knowing how. They seemed impressed that they were being covered by a journalist from Portugal; at that time, people barely knew where Portugal was, in my early time in the UK. *A Bola* had given me an ID card with my photo on it, and showing that card was the only thing I had to do when I turned up at the door of the stadium. People at the club were very welcoming, in the Scottish manner, and they just let me come in. I ended up being a bit of a friend to all of them, I went to all the games, and I even went to training sometimes, including going down to Seamill to cover their preparations for the Lisbon final."

Miguel explains that his initial contact with *A Bola* was supplied to him by an old school friend, Jorge Schnitzer, who in the mid-1960s was a radio sports reporter with the long-standing Portuguese radio station Rádio Renascença (owned by the Roman Catholic Church), and who was himself to conduct a brief interview with the match referee for the 1967 final, Kurt Tschenscher (published in *A Bola* on May 27th 1967). In fact, as time went on, Miguel's brief was not purely to cover Celtic: the newspaper permitted him on one occasion to go to Ajax to interview a youthful Johan Cruyff; he was also dispatched to Northern Ireland to research Linfield before they faced Vitória Setúbal in the Inter-Cities Fairs' Cup in 1968-69; and he also travelled to Liverpool to interview Emlyn Hughes in preparation for a tie between Liverpool and the same Portuguese opponents the following season. Clearly, therefore, he was considered to be doing a good job for the newspaper.

As already noted, he was well connected, even before he came to Scotland, and he was to use these connections to good effect in Celtic's cause. When he was asked about journalistic objectivity, his reply indicated that, while he sought to represent factual matters correctly and reliably, there was no doubt where his loyalties lay, not least as the final approached: "It began professionally, just supplying to *A Bola* factual information about the players, how much they weighed, things like that, and reports on the games they played, but as they got closer to Lisbon, I have to admit that I was trying to win local support for them for the final in Portugal. I did all I could so that Portuguese people who went to the stadium would be for Celtic and not for Inter. About 10,000 Celtic supporters went to Lisbon, I think (I wrote that in the newspaper), and my friend Denis was one of them, and I think his brother Jimmy too, and you can imagine the rest: the party they had, and they ended up kissing the grass. In terms of when I thought that Celtic would win, it was never about thinking that: it was more a matter of hoping they would win. In that team, and in that coach, Jock Stein, who was a magnificent coach and a magnificent man, there was a soul, a victorious spirit which made me believe that it was possible. On the other side, there was Inter, who were a monster at that time. For them, it wasn't their first final: it was juniors against the experienced seniors, and it was Celtic's spirit which won the game, I think. Did I influence people in Portugal? I would rather be modest and say not a lot, but I am sure that some Portuguese people, above all those who supported Sporting, were influenced by my articles. Every day *A Bola* came out there was an article (and often a spread) about Celtic, and because of the similarity of their colours with Sporting, there maybe was a tendency to go with Celtic. Also, it's easier to create support for David than for Goliath. Inter were very well known, and there was maybe greater football rivalry between Portuguese and Italians than Portuguese and Scots. I couldn't say for sure. Everyone interested in football was reading *A Bola*.

At that time *A Bola* was read more than the *Diário de Notícias* or *O Século,* and *Record* was much less important, having a much lower circulation, maybe half of *A Bola,* and so I think people who read it had a certain tendency to take Celtic's side."

So behind the apparent statement of humility in these words, Miguel does actually assert the importance of his work: his articles in *A Bola* were given considerable prominence by the paper (certainly the closer one gets to the date of the final), and his writing displays in-depth insights into the history of the club, the genuine quality of Scottish football at the time (he also gives some coverage to the very good Rangers team of the time, as well as the Scottish national team), but his main focus was clearly on the merits of the Celtic players. Considering that Inter were widely acknowledged as the outstanding team in Europe at the time and relatively few people would have known much about Celtic across Europe, his efforts in giving publicity to the team were absolutely invaluable. And one of the merits which he saw in the team appears to have been precisely the down-to-earth openness of the players, by way of contrast with the godlike aura surrounding the superstars of Inter. He talks about the friendly reception which he found within the club: "Yes, there was Gemmell and especially Craig, who was training to become a dentist. I had the greatest feelings of warmth with them, and with Billy McNeill, the captain, as well as Steve Chalmers, who wasn't a regular in the team at the time, but who was one of the really good forwards that they had. The photo of me with him [Chalmers] shows him with a slight injury to his ankle, which he had got in the Scottish League Cup final in October 1969, and they were concerned about that, which is why he has one foot with no shoe on, and that is also why Jock Stein is sitting next him too." (In fact, this turned out to be a fracture, a much more serious injury than was realised at the time, and it ruled Chalmers out for the remainder of the season.)

"As far as the players were concerned, I liked 'wee' Johnstone, who was like a very devil, and I really liked Bertie Auld, who had a very 'Latin' style of play. He thought about space, he didn't just 'kick and run', and he even looked Latin, with his dark hair. He reminded me of Travassos of Sporting Lisbon, who in my opinion had the same sort of style, as I said in my reports, and he was the great hero of my youth, even if he didn't like me very much as a coach! I didn't maintain the friendship with the players: it was a professional friendship. I had the liberty to contact them when I wanted and interview them, but not outside the professional arena. I didn't go to the cinema with them or anything like that. My friend Denis, who has been my friend for nearly fifty years and who was an art teacher, is the only friend I still have from those days. The players weren't used to a foreign journalist turning up nearly every week from the other end of the world, and since I wrote for a newspaper which was beginning to become known overseas at that time, I showed them the articles I had written with the headlines in big letters. The players ended up enjoying seeing that and thanked me for it. A journalist is supposed to be neutral, but by the end I wasn't really neutral. I wanted 'my Celtic' to win, and with all humility I think my reports helped to make Celtic a team that Portuguese people going to see the final would like before they actually went there."

Of course, for a Portuguese audience who would have seen, and known, very little of Scottish football before the final, Miguel's articles had to resort to comparisons with some of their own stars, and he selected his models carefully, recalling, for example, his comparisons in *A Bola* of Jimmy Johnstone to António Simões, the left-winger of both the great Benfica team of the early 1960s and the Portuguese team which had reached the World Cup semi-finals in England in 1966: "Regarding Johnstone and Simões, he (Simões) was also tiny, and even if he wasn't a red-head he was lighter-skinned than someone like Travassos. He had that trick of feinting (even if he was a left-winger and Johnstone was a right-winger) and that speed and facility and technique which was a great trump-card in the football of those days. Wee Johnstone was like a mouse who could dribble with extraordinary ease, who could turn and who could run really fast. Simões was the same in the style of play – maybe less so in the physical aspect."

John Clark, meantime, was compared to Vicente, of Belenenses, who had marked Pelé out of the game during the World Cup in England the previous year, and Miguel's praise for Bertie Auld is based around one of the great heroes of Portuguese football before the era of television, José Travassos, an integral member of the great 'Five Violins' forward line of Sporting Lisbon in the late 1940s and early 1950s (so called because of the sweetness of their combined play), and who had also, of course, been Miguel's own coach in his time at Sporting's youth section: "Vicente was an international player who had a foot amputated, but during his career I admired him for his calm and thoughtful play, and John Clark had an attitude which was very much like Vicente's. I didn't make those comparisons to create favouritism. I did it more to explain to the readers as well as I could what Celtic were like. Bertie Auld had that style of play and even the same appearance as Travassos, and so maybe when people read this they liked Auld more than some midfielder for Inter."

All of this is understandable, but the degree of enthusiasm and commitment which was required of Miguel to carry out his 'missionary' work on behalf of Celtic should not be underestimated. This was not like today, when social media enables text to be sent across the globe instantly. The method adopted would be unthinkable now: "I remember I had to read my texts out over the phone; a time was set for the call in advance, I would wait for it, and then the British telephone operator would link me up to the person on the telephone desk at *A Bola*. There was no fax then, there wasn't anything in those ancient times!"

Unfortunately, Miguel himself did not get to savour Celtic's greatest day in person in his native country. When asked about what he did on May 25th 1967, he says: "Regarding the final, I was certainly very sorry not to be going to Lisbon, but my student 'allowance' didn't permit me any great adventures, especially in a month when (in theory) I was supposed to be concentrating on my studies. But I should also admit that, although by that stage I was already a passionate Celtic fan, I didn't quite believe in them winning against the monsters of Inter. *A Bola* didn't stop me from going, and maybe they did actually prefer me to stay in Glasgow to comment on the reaction there [which he did in the edition of May 27th]. The truth is that in Lisbon they had their established journalists, and they didn't need me. I remember watching the match in my student flat. But it's all a long time ago now. I don't remember much, but I went to celebrate in a sort of private club near to my flat, the St. Mungo's Centenary Club in Great Western Road."

One further important question, however, involves the nickname 'The Lisbon Lions'. This term was used by Ken Gallacher in a *Daily Record* article on March 20th 1964, when Sporting Lisbon were one of the semi-finalists against whom Celtic could have been drawn in the European Cup-Winners' Cup (which Sporting went on to win that season, beating Celtic's conquerors, MTK Budapest, in the final). Gallacher's preview of Celtic's potential opponents explicitly referred to them as 'The Lisbon Lions', an allusion to the club crest which features a lion rampant drawn from the coat of arms of one of the aristocratic founding families of the club, the Castelo Brancos. (By coincidence the term 'Lisbon Lions' was also used by one English journalist to refer to the England team which beat Portugal 10-0 at the Jamor Stadium twenty years precisely to the day before Celtic's triumph there.) So is it possible, particularly in view of the identical shirts worn by Celtic and Sporting, that the nickname which has become synonymous with Celtic's greatest ever side was coined by a Portuguese journalist looking for a new set of British sporting heroes, or perhaps by a Scot who noticed the lion on the Sporting club emblem while he was there and thought of the traditional Scottish (Lion Rampant) flag? Miguel certainly thinks that this is a strong possibility: why would Portuguese sports journalists observing the match *not* have thought of a link to the team from their own city, after all, when Celtic wore the same colours? "Absolutely. Whose idea it was, I don't know. It would be presumptuous of me to say that it was me who gave them that name. I made it my intention to try to transmit the message that

Celtic were like Sporting, but regarding the name 'The Lisbon Lions', I can't really say who invented it for the victorious Celtic team. The parallel between the lion on the Sporting club crest and the fact that the Celtic club crest doesn't have any animal makes me think there is some connection."

When Miguel was asked about his feelings about the modern Celtic, co-author David Frier was surprised by the nature of his answer, even half a century after his time in Glasgow: "Yes, I absolutely am still a Celtic fan. I receive the club newsletter every week, the *Celtic View*. I have Celtic shirts here, I have a Celtic scarf which I bought from the club website, and other knick-knacks, pens and things. If there were a game between Sporting and Celtic, I think Sporting would be closer to my heart, it's inevitable - when I was just ten I was already listening to radio reports on their games in that wonderful period when they won lots of titles. But I'm sure that if Celtic won I would be nearly as happy. There isn't any third club in my heart – there are only two. I have never gone back to Glasgow since that last visit in the late 60s. Maybe some day we can meet and go to a match at Parkhead? I always dream of going to see a match, even if the stadium has been renovated and is so different from the one I knew."

So the club acquired a lifelong admirer in 1966-67, and the affection for Celtic has never left him. It is impossible to quantify the 'Paiva Couceiro' factor precisely, but there can be little doubt that Celtic owe him thanks for raising the local profile of the club in the run-up to the biggest match in their history. His in-depth reports and his 'boosting' of some of the team's key players meant that Celtic were never going to walk alone when they stepped out on to the turf of the National Stadium on May 25th 1967. There were approximately 10-15,000 Scots there, but there were also many Portuguese who favoured Celtic because of the dedicated efforts of a young student who just happened to find himself in the right place at the right time.

CHAPTER 9

"And the Celts were bound for Lisbon town, on the Twenty-Fifth of May..."

For many of the Celtic supporters who travelled to Portugal there was a large element of that happy-go-lucky, spontaneous holiday spirit characteristic of an expedition which was conducted as part of a large community. Britain was on the cusp of the era of mass, cheap air travel, and many supporters had never been abroad before, and so the prospect of an unpredictable and mysterious journey to a sunnier, unfamiliar country for the biggest match in the club's history must have seemed a glamorous one, even if it was one which stretched many a household budget to the limit. And everyone knows the multitude of stories about improvised travel arrangements in buses, taxi cabs, charter aircraft and private cars (notably the 'Celticade') which have entered the mythology of Lisbon 1967.

Scottish press coverage of the host country itself, however, was superficial to the point of being virtually non-existent. By 1967 Portugal had become established as one of the leading footballing countries in Europe: the national team had only been eliminated in the 1966 World Cup semi-finals by the hosts and eventual winners, England, and many considered the Portuguese unlucky to have lost at that stage. Eusébio had been the star player of the tournament, with an astonishing nine goals, and his club side, Benfica, had won the European Cup twice and been losing finalists on two further occasions in the first half of the decade. Meanwhile, Sporting Lisbon had won the European Cup-Winners' Cup in 1964, so that it was easy to see why UEFA would have regarded Lisbon as a logical venue for a final. As we shall see in a later chapter, however, the path which led to Lisbon hosting the final was a complex, twisting one, which leads right into the heart of 1960s football politics, an arena in which both Portugal and Scotland were small players: there is a delicious irony, then, in Inter having met their footballing nemesis in the Portuguese capital, partly as a result of their own attempts to bend the tournament towards their own ends two years earlier, but the present chapter will focus on some of the local circumstances which contributed in their own way to the hallowed event which Lisbon is in Celtic's history.

The photos of a sunny day in Lisbon, an elegant city of "statued squares" and a myriad of colours on display exemplified by its red roofs, yellow trams and green buses, mask a country which was not at ease with itself in 1967: Portugal had been under the rule of an authoritarian dictator, António Oliveira de Salazar, since the early 1930s, and the wealth and opulence of a multi-continental overseas Empire (reflected in some of the magnificent, tree-lined avenues and impressive churches, palaces and municipal buildings of the capital) co-existed with levels of poverty and illiteracy which were amongst the very worst in Europe. Mass migration to wealthier countries in northern Europe - often illegal, and sometimes undertaken to avoid conscription into an army which was fighting an unpopular colonial war in Africa and which was eventually to overthrow the regime in 1974 - existed side by side with a sense of economic and social stagnation arising from the lack of any clearly identifiable alternative to Salazar's regime. Meanwhile censorship of the press and repressive police action ensured that the country continued to function in a largely compliant fashion. Nonetheless, questions regarding the future of the country were becoming more insistent with every year that passed as the leader became older and seemingly refused to countenance any serious consideration of his own succession. His 'New State' (where all political parties were prohibited) and his own adept political touch in avoiding awkward compromises enabled his government to maintain a relatively closed, largely rural, low-wage society which resisted the large-scale consumer development of most of the rest of Western Europe in the twenty years following the end of the Second World War. Most importantly, however, the country's relative isolation from mainstream European politics had enabled it to maintain its African colonies, even as the other European colonial powers (Britain, France and Belgium) were divesting themselves of Empire. It was the possession of these colonies which allowed Portugal to claim as its own such fine footballers as Eusébio and his Benfica teammates Mário Coluna and José Águas (the latter came from Angola, while the other two players were born and raised in Mozambique), but by the 1960s Portugal found itself embroiled in an increasingly futile and costly colonial war against nationalist rebels in Angola, Mozambique and Guiné-Bissau. The undoubted successes on the football field were therefore increasingly being used by the government for propaganda purposes, both at home and abroad (for example, photographs of Eusébio in military uniform were particularly valuable, since the country's outstanding player offered an exaggerated image of Mozambican integration into national life, which he was grateful to accept in return for the opportunity to make a very good living in mainland Portugal).

By the mid-1960s Portugal was coming under increasing international pressure to renounce its colonial policies, and relations with the United Kingdom were under particular strain, as the British government was unhappy with the use of Mozambican ports to deliver oil to the breakaway government of Rhodesia, led by Ian Smith (this is amply documented in files held at the National Archives in Kew, in London); meanwhile, successive resolutions at the United Nations had called on Portugal to decolonise in Africa. The official Portuguese position, however, was that its overseas territories were not colonies, but an integral part of national territory, and therefore that there was no colonial situation to be addressed. The maintenance of this position required the country to show itself off as a 'normal' country, conducting business as usual. While many Celtic supporters who went to Lisbon in 1967 may have been struck by relative poverty on the streets and perhaps even by the sight of maimed war veterans with limbs missing (one at least of whom, judging by one photo, was pictured at the *Estádio Nacional* selling tickets for the final), most of them would certainly have been unaware that this was a country at war. Officially there was no war, and the conflict was kept very much overseas, with reports in the media using terminology relating to 'terrorists' on the one side being 'pacified' by Portuguese troops on the other. At home, however, political and social tensions were very much in the air: 1961 had seen a number of embarrassing demonstrations of opposition to the supposed government of national unity; in 1965 the prominent dissident General Humberto Delgado was assassinated in Spain by operatives of the Portuguese secret police in conjunction with Franco's agents; and, with large numbers of Portuguese migrants working abroad (in France, Germany and the United States, amongst other countries), there was a growing awareness within Portugal of poor economic conditions, as well as of the curtailment of personal freedoms.

If the mid to late 1960s elsewhere would come to be defined by the Beatles, the 1967 'Summer of love' and growing movements to secure freedoms for women and ethnic minorities, Portugal (in common with its only land neighbour, Spain) was still a largely closed, restrictive and hierarchical society, and communications to London from the British Embassy in Lisbon at the time speculate freely about what would happen to the country once its now ageing ruler retired or died. The uncertainty regarding future paths for the country was also reflected in the cautious opening up of the Portuguese economy to foreign investment and imports: on the one hand, successful musical groups such as the Beatles and the Rolling Stones achieved success in Portugal, as they did elsewhere in Europe, and in the 1960s women began to make some inroads into the employment market, beyond their traditional roles in professions such as nursing, cleaning and school-teaching. Nonetheless, another mark of modernity, Coca Cola, remained banned in the country until after the 1974 Revolution (crowd photos from the Lisbon final show the prominence of the nationally-produced soft drink *Sumol* on sale instead), but advertisements in the Portuguese press at the time indicate a growth in marketing of consumer products such as motor cars, designer watches and televisions and the marketing of many of the same films as were being shown elsewhere in Europe at the time. In Lisbon, those who were not interested in football could have gone to the cinemas on the day of the final to watch, for example, Natalie Wood and Robert Redford starring in a film adaptation of Tennessee Williams's *This Property Must be Condemned*, Rock Hudson's *Seconds*, or George Segal, Alec Guinness and Max von Sydow in *The Quiller Memorandum*. And in 1966, the Portuguese state broadcaster, RTP, had finally become members of the Eurovision network (membership of which was an absolutely necessary condition for hosting the European Cup final) after dipping its toes in the water by making its debut in the Eurovision Song Contest two years earlier. In spite of decades of aloofness, when Portugal had been declaring itself to be somewhat distant from a Europe divided between speculative market capitalism and repressive Communism, it was now turning towards Europe, well aware of the growing possibility (indeed, necessity) of cashing in on its pleasant climate and sunny beaches and allowing its own middle classes to increase their spending power. One advertisement in the government's Lisbon tourist office in May 1967 promoted the country as follows: "Good food, wine, and entertainment – we have it all. And all at the lowest prices in Europe." Another used a description "The only foreign country left in Europe", which hinted at a national inferiority complex while drawing attention, rather obliquely, to Portugal as being an under-patronised holiday destination in comparison with more established tourist hubs in Spain, France and Italy.

For a city like Lisbon to stage the European Cup final, then, required the city and the country to be put on a show for the world to see, but the Portuguese Football Federation (FPF) only really woke up to this fact as the date of the final approached, as we shall see. This was not directly an issue for the government, as Salazar was far less concerned with football than he was with a Papal visit to the Catholic shrine at Fátima in mid-May 1967, an event which highlighted Portugal's predominantly agrarian society and the country's 'underdeveloped' image, with reports that many (presumably poor rural workers) of the estimated one million pilgrims to the shrine had walked miles and miles with swollen and bloody feet and braved the rain as they sloshed through the mud, ending up spending the night out of doors on the eve of the ceremony. John Quinn of Glasgow's *Evening Times*, who travelled later that month with the 'Celticade', would recall a Portugal of country roads from which could be seen one evening

79

"homeward-bound farm workers, men with pairs of oxen and women leading *burros* laden with wood and the day's produce from the fields."

Since the Pope's denunciation of Portugal's African policies had drawn attention to strained relations with the Vatican, one can see why the civil authorities were determined to use the football match as a means of projecting a better image of Portugal abroad. The impatience of the broader Portuguese population with a seemingly never-ending dictatorship perhaps contributed in some degree to the support shown to Celtic by the locals. A perusal of the end-of-year report to the Foreign Office written by the British Ambassador in January 1968 (stored in the National Archives at Kew) reveals that anything British was likely to be well received in the country at the time, since Britain represented both a democratic tradition and, in the existing climate, a source of opposition to Salazar's government. So, while there was some tension between Britain and Portugal at the time, all concerned in Portugal had an interest in ensuring that their Scottish visitors had as positive an experience as possible, as evidenced by Alex Cameron of the *Scottish Daily Mail* reporting that the police had been told to act as courteously as possible towards Scottish visitors. Looking back in 2007, Celtic fan Bernie Boyle was quoted as identifying another important contributory factor to the welcome that the visitors enjoyed: "The majority of Celtic fans were Catholics, so the chapels were packed and it helped win over the Lisbon people. They were expecting cold-hearted Scots and there we were, not only singing and dancing in the main square, but attending Mass too." John Quinn would recall from his travels through Portugal en route to the final that the citizens of Lisbon, indeed the entire country of Portugal, took the green and white army to their hearts: "They had never seen anything like it as the Scots fans invaded the town centres, taking over cafes and restaurants with their singing and dancing." Add the extra ingredient of lingering local resentment for Helenio Herrera's Inter Milan following that club's controversial victory over Benfica in the 1965 final, and the stage was indeed set for May 1967 to become a truly memorable month for the Celtic support.

The stadium chosen to host the final was to be for those fans a revelation, but the *Estádio Nacional* (National Stadium), located some ten miles from Lisbon city centre, was already something of a relic or 'white elephant' in 1967, being rarely used for major sporting events: it was also a surprise choice for this match, even for Portuguese commentators, who had expected it to be held at either Benfica's *Estádio da Luz* or Sporting's Alvalade Stadium, where Bertie Auld had played for Scotland in a friendly international in 1959. Both of these venues were closer to the city itself and Benfica's stadium had a larger capacity than the 54,000 maximum of the National Stadium, which tended to be used only for matches involving the Portuguese national team or for the Portuguese Cup final (now it is the latter only). When the Portuguese federation declared to UEFA its interest in holding the 1967 final, it had originally mentioned only the same two clubs' stadia as options, according to a report in *A Bola*, on February 11th 1967. Something, then, clearly changed minds between the choice (in summer 1966) of Lisbon for the final and February 1967, when the definitive venue was announced.

The National Stadium, positioned at the head of the broad Jamor valley that sweeps down to the Atlantic, was (and still is) a magnificent and impressive, indeed enchanting, arena, and the playing surface was of the very highest standard, with carefully selected grass sown to create an optimum playing surface. In fact, the pitch was praised in advance of the final by both coaches, with Jock Stein (quoted in *A Bola* of May 13th 1967) saying that he had inspected it in 1963 on a previous visit to Lisbon for a Fairs Cities' Cup play-off against Valencia as manager of Dunfermline Athletic, while Helenio Herrera, already aware of the venue from his time with Belenenses in the 1950s, was reported in the same paper five days later to have remarked that there was no better pitch in the world than the Jamor (the stadium itself is often referred to by the name of the river valley), in an evident attempt to court local favour. Ironically, as it turned out, he was also quoted elsewhere as saying that "It is impossible to play badly on such a surface." More presciently, Desmond Hackett of the *Daily Express* said on the morning of the match that the turf was "a Wembley-style playing area where sound stamina is as good as having a Eusebio or Pele in the side." Yet it was in other respects a venue unsuitable for major matches: the media facilities were limited, the location was a long way out of the city (although there was a railway station in operation at the stadium on big match occasions until late 1979), the seating described by one Celtic fan as "just concrete steps with an extra charge if you wanted a cushion", and – most strikingly of all – one side of the stadium was left wide open. For the purposes of the European Cup final - and only after the deficient press facilities and the lack of cover were highlighted in *Record* - a temporary, rather small, press stand holding a maximum of 250 journalists was erected belatedly on that side of the pitch (telephones were installed only a day or two before the final), a layout which created an unusual, indeed probably unique, assymetrical backdrop for the biggest fixture of the European club season. As it happened, the temporary stand was not big enough to hold all the accredited pressmen, with the result that some had to be accommodated elsewhere. Further evidence that, between them, the FPF and UEFA had been caught off-guard by the level of interest in the final came a week before the match when the FPF president, Justino Pinheiro Machado, was obliged to apply to the mayor of Lisbon for an extra fifty places to be reserved at an eve-of-final civic reception for UEFA and FPF dignitaries, match officials, foreign pressmen, and directors of the competing clubs (Bob Kelly and Desmond White represented Celtic).

The reason for the apparently strange situation of one side of the stadium being open was not, as some writers have claimed, the result of the stadium builders running out of money to complete the project. In fact, memos written by the architects in the 1940s make it very clear that one side of the arena was specifically designed to be left open as part of the general conception of the stadium as a site for Portuguese sportsmen and women to escape from the increasingly unhealthy aspects of urban life and to exercise and train in the pure air of the Jamor valley. It was intended to be a symbol of the regime's view of sport as a unifying aspect of national culture, to be conducted in an environment where both athletes and spectators could "feel in harmony with the spirit of the nation." The design of the stadium had been influenced by both Berlin's Olympic Stadium (the site of the 1936 'Nazi' Games, a monument to Fascist power) and by the Ancient Greek philosophy of integrating the construction of arenas, either sporting or theatrical, with the natural surroundings; at those 1936 Games there were rumours, probably fostered by the Salazar regime, of Portugal (with the National Stadium as the centrepiece) hosting the 1940 Games, but the advent of World War Two put an end to such an eventuality. In a purely domestic context, under the dictatorship, performances of such ritual sports as gymnastics and athletics were intended to be carried out in an environment where (on the one side) the participants could see themselves within the forested Portuguese countryside and, on the other, they could see (and be seen by) their political leaders and other dignitaries who were sitting in the V.I.P. area (*Tribuna de honra*) flanked by marble colonnades, a more aesthetically pleasing and dramatic construction than, for example, its British equivalent (the directors' box) and one where in 1967 Billy McNeill was to receive the European Cup from the hands of President Américo Tomás. In addition, the open side of the arena was intended to permit the parade of large demonstrations of national solidarity into the stadium by organisations such as the *Mocidade Portuguesa* (or 'Portuguese Youth'), a rather more militarised version of the Boy Scouts, with a strongly nationalistic flavour overlaying all of their activities. Documentary film footage of the opening ceremony in June 1944 makes it abundantly clear, then, that football was a secondary consideration in the original design of this arena, and the sight of an Olympic torch at this event was meant to signify that Portugal, a nation at peace in a world being devastated by conflict, was a worthy candidate to hold the very biggest events in sport. (The stadium took some time to shake off the taint of its associations with fascism: for example, between 1975 and 1977, in the early years of the 'Carnation Revolution', Portuguese cup finals were played elsewhere before reverting to the National Stadium after football fans had made it clear that they enjoyed their days out there: its idyllic surroundings have proved to be an ideal spot for picnickers, lending what one writer has described as an "air of holiday and unreality not usually associated with a football ground.")

Even in a right-wing, authoritarian country such as Portugal, however, displays of fervent enthusiasm for the regime as outlined above fell completely out of fashion with the defeat of Nazi Germany, and, though the stadium was used for big occasions such as the annual Portuguese Cup Final and had hosted the very first ever match in the European Cup (a 3-3 draw between Sporting Lisbon and Partizan Belgrade, played on September 4th 1955, while Sporting's new stadium was still under construction), the rise of the bigger clubs and their increasing professionalisation during the course of the 1950s led them, one after another, to construct larger stadia specifically designed with football in mind and in more convenient locations. Put quite simply, the dressing rooms, the media facilities and the other peripheral facilities (even for a 1960s stadium) were far more fit for purpose at the Luz or the Alvalade than they were at the National Stadium: both Benfica and Sporting had regularly staged matches attracting significant foreign interest, not least Benfica's home European Cup match against Manchester United in March 1966, which had attracted significant interest across Europe and where extra media facilities had been laid on, to the apparent satisfaction of all concerned.

So why was the National Stadium chosen in preference to better equipped stadia owned by the city's two leading club sides? On December 15th 1966, *A Bola* (which seems to have had an inside track to information from the Portuguese Football Federation, the FPF) announced the definitive date for the match: Thursday May 25th 1967. When the venue was then confirmed as the National Stadium in the same paper on February 9th 1967, the newspaper went out of its way to stress the magnificence of the surroundings, while also raising a more practical consideration: "the sunshine will contribute to the festivities, with the additional advantage for the organisers that the National Stadium does not belong to any club, so that there is no problem raised by having to offer tickets to club members." Subsequent articles which alluded to the choice of venue generally talked up the positive publicity which could be generated for Portuguese football and for the country as a whole from holding the match at the symbolic home of national sport. A local newspaper, the *Jornal de Oeiras*, would not even have entertained any debate about the venue, proudly describing the *Estádio Nacional* in its edition of May 18th 2004 as "the stadium for the whole Portuguese people." Yet in some respects this choice was still found surprising at the time.

The date and time for the match clearly prompted some considered thought: originally, when (in July 1966) the same paper had announced that the 1967 Final would be played in Lisbon, it had indicated that it would be played on Wednesday May 24th. This was not the first time that the final would be played on a Thursday rather than the traditional Wednesday. This had also been the case with the 1957 final between Real Madrid and Fiorentina, played at the Bernabeu, as well as with the 1965 final between Inter and Benfica at the San Siro, with one Giuliano Sarti playing in goal for the Italian team on both occasions. The official reason offered for the choice of the Thursday (in *A Bola*, of February 11th 1967) was to avoid a clash with three full internationals taking place on May 24th (one of which, that between England and Spain, was watched by the Celtic players on television as a form of relaxation on the eve of their own match). This prioritisation of friendly internationals may seem unlikely now, but it was not so unusual at that time: UEFA had originally been hesitant about the introduction of the Champions' Cup in the mid-1950s and had, in fact, insisted that it was not called by names such as 'European Championship' in order to prevent the gloss being taken away from their own projected tournament for national teams, the European Nations Cup, which did not get underway until September 1958.

Nonetheless, the choice of the Thursday simultaneously supports the idea of a decisive preference in favour of the National Stadium. Thursday May 25th was the Catholic Feast of Corpus Christi, and in a country where Church and state formed a close symbolic alliance, this was a public holiday. Scheduling the match for that Thursday, therefore, permitted those Portuguese spectators who had to work to attend the match without leaving work early, the chosen kick-off time of 5.30 p.m. being deemed a necessity to allow for the possibility of extra time being played in order to complete the match before darkness fell, since at that time the stadium possessed no floodlights. Both Benfica's and Sporting's grounds did have floodlights, so those venues would have been available either on the 24th or the 25th, and the match could then have kicked off at the usual mid-evening time. As indicated above, however, this might have meant offering subsidised tickets to club members of Sporting or Benfica, and there is evidence that the FPF was under some pressure from both UEFA and the Portuguese government to maximise income from the match. The newly-appointed Director of the National Stadium, Eduardo Trigo, had stated that "We must derive greater returns from the long-term investment which the National Stadium represents" (as reported in *A Bola*, October 20th 1966).

This government decree, coming as it did in the same year as the prestigious inauguration of the Salazar Bridge over the Tagus – an impressive construction remarkably similar in design to the Forth Road Bridge - carried significant weight. Portugal was keen to impress the world in general with the beauty and magnificence of its stadium and it also wished to lay on a reminder to its own people that it could stage major modern events as well as any other country, but in its own way. Portugal was to be seen to be different from the rest of Europe in some ways, but in no sense was it to be seen to be inferior or technologically backward. The same report in *A Bola* which discussed the change of date to the Thursday also remarked that the National Stadium had the advantage over club stadia in that there was no pitch-side advertising: this final was to be played instead in a setting where sport would be celebrated for its own sake; the commercial vulgarity of advertisements (which were looked on with some disdain in official circles, even if they were tolerated as a necessary evil in a now more market-oriented economy) would not be allowed to sully this spectacle; and, yet at the same time, full ticket prices could be charged to the public, with no advantage being given to members of Sporting over Benfica or vice versa. During the period leading up to the final (and even after it), *A Bola* was to continually remind its readership of the magnificent setting of the National Stadium, whose spectacular visual appeal did indeed captivate spectators and journalists alike, and the regime's long-standing suspicion of demonstrating explicit club affiliations (which had been quite overtly regarded as being detrimental to feelings of national unity in the 1940s) may have led to a desire to avoid any suggestion of favouring one of the capital's leading clubs over the other.

For better or for worse, however, the final was to take place at the National Stadium, and there can be no doubt that the spectacular visual appearance of the arena greatly impressed everyone in attendance, enabling the FPF to boast about the "verdant framing of its colourful scenery, in an atmosphere of joyous sporting enthusiasm" being projected in TV images throughout Europe and in acres of newsprint throughout the world "in the most glowing terms, giving plenty of positive propaganda for our country." Unquestionably, as the coverage by those same media outlets made clear, that atmosphere was greatly enhanced by the thousands who had travelled from Scotland and beyond and who were captivated by the beautiful Portuguese capital, described by one writer in the following terms: "A place of magnificently elegant, tree-lined streets and finely-proportioned, gleaming buildings, and – off the main avenues – side streets sweep gracefully upwards, while everywhere there are enticing bars and restaurants." A travel agent's dream. No wonder that in an interview with Ken Gallacher of the *Daily Record* in May 1975, Celtic captain Billy McNeill made the following observation: "Somehow I still feel that the fans who followed us there had the best of that game. They took part in the fairytale just as much as we did. They helped make the game, the whole cavalier

85

[misprint for 'carnival'?] atmosphere stemmed from them and their belief in us."

For the club and its fans, then, the *Estádio Nacional* will forever be Celtic's Elysian Fields.

1. "Backs to the Wall!" Billy McNeill heads clear during a dogged defensive display by Celtic in the European Cup semi-final second leg vs. Dukla in Prague in April 1967.

2. Celtic players training on a side pitch in the National Stadium complex shortly after arrival in Lisbon on May 23rd 1967. Clearly visible here are (left to right): Cattanach, Gallagher, Wallace, and behind the latter are Auld (partially hidden by Wallace), Lennox, Cushley, Gemmell (to right of Cushley in photo), Murdoch and Chalmers.

3. On the eve: Jock Stein gives a press conference on the pitch at the National Stadium after Celtic's training session there on the morning of May 24th 1967.

4. Celtic players (from left to right, O'Neill, Lennox, Gallagher and Young) mingle with a group of fans (believed to be from Bathgate) on the pitch at the National Stadium after a training session on the morning of May 24th 1967. Note in the background the small cabins with restricted view of the pitch used by television commentators during the match.

5. The teams and match officials line up before the match. Note in the background the dramatic profile of the Presidential Area, where the trophy was presented after the match, and the seating area below that.

6. *A Bola* reporter Miguel de Paiva Couceiro chats with Steve Chalmers in the Celtic dressing room after the 1969 League Cup Final victory over St. Johnstone. Note that the player is not wearing a shoe on one foot after the fracture sustained during the match. Jock Stein sits anxiously to one side.

7. Sandro Mazzola sends Ronnie Simpson the wrong way to score Inter's early goal from the penalty spot.

8. Bobby Murdoch retrieves the ball (also missing from the original print) from the Celtic net after the Inter Milan goal, while the spirit of his team-mates is demonstrated in the distance as Auld and Clark continue to dispute the penalty award with the referee.

9. Jimmy Johnstone turns Inter defender Burgnich inside out during the first half of the final. Note the temporary press stand erected specially for this match in the background.

10. Sarti and his defenders strive desperately to repel a Celtic attack in the first half, with Corso, a forward (no. 11), giving a helping hand.

11. A side view of the same incident, with Steve Chalmers (no. 9) to the fore for Celtic.

12. Jock Stein and Helenio Herrera in an angry exchange as they leave the pitch at half time. Witnesses following behind them are Dottore Chiesa, an advisor to Inter (left), and club doctor Angiolino Quarenghi.

13. The breakthrough! A thunderbolt shot from Tommy Gemmell (partially hidden) rockets towards the roof of the net for the equaliser.

14. Celtic players surround Gemmell in celebration after his goal. Note the despair on the face of the two Inter defenders (Bedin looks on as Picchi is rising from the turf after failing to block Gemmell's shot) and that virtually everyone in the crowd appears to be celebrating the goal. The Celtic number 10 is Auld, and number 5 is a relieved-looking Billy McNeill.

15. Herrera, pictured on the bench between two Inter officials, Dottore Chiesa and Angiolino Quarenghi, watches his hopes of a third European Cup drift away, late in the second half of the match.

SARTI, DOS «GLOBETROTTERS»...

LENNOX OBSERVA, INCRÉDULO E DESESPERADO, SARTI NEGAR-LHE UMA VEZ MAIS O GOLO. PEGANDO À BOLA DE FORMA TÃO MALABARISTA COMO SÓ É HÁBITO VER PEGAR NELA AOS BASQUETEBOLISTAS DO «HARLEM GLOBETROTTERS»

16. Yet another astonishing save by Sarti, as he clutches the ball one-handed from a close-in Murdoch header during the second half of the Final in an action described by the newspaper caption as being worthy of the Harlem Globetrotters basketball team.

17. Penalty, surely! But referee Tschenscher did not get as clear a sight as this photographer of Sarti grabbing Wallace by the legs during the latter stages of the final.

18. And it's there! Steve Chalmers turns away in celebration after turning Murdoch's shot into the net for the winning goal. Jimmy Johnstone begins to raise his arms in celebration, while Sarti and two Inter defenders look on in despair.

19. Celtic fans break out into celebrations during the final, either for a goal or at the final whistle. The newspaper caption does not specify the moment.

20. A kilted supporter runs onto the pitch to join the Celtic players in celebrating Chalmers' winning goal.

21. It's all over! Fans swarm onto the pitch in celebration at the final whistle.

22. An impromptu *ceilidh* on the pitch at the National Stadium as these Celtic supporters dance for joy at the end of the match.

23. A bare-chested Billy McNeill is lifted high by supporters on the pitch at the end of the match.

24. Billy McNeill, with the assistance of police officers, makes his way through the crowds to prepare for the trophy presentation.

25. Billy McNeill holds aloft the new European Cup trophy.

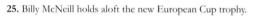

26. Scenes of celebration amidst the chaos after the match as a young fan appears to be holding the giant trophy towards John Clark for the latter to have a drink of champagne from it. Note on the right-hand side a fan holding a Sporting Lisbon cap with the club's lion emblem visible.

27. A satirical cartoon by Francisco Zambujal published in *A Bola* on 27th May 1967 depicts Helenio Herrera having his throat burnt by whisky offered to him by a kilted Celtic supporter. The supporter taunts him by saying "So your throat was burnt by two little goals/swigs?", playing on the similarity of the two words in Portuguese. Many papers across Europe could not resist the opportunity to revel in Herrera's downfall in Lisbon.

28. How *A Bola* saw the final: the front page of the paper on 27th May 1967 prints the word 'Celtic' in tartan letters, with the subheadings "Promise fulfilled! A Historic Day! A V for Victory in the Green Symphony", while another article further down the page carries the headline "Thank you, Scotland, for the service you have done to real football." The photo at the foot of the page is the winning goal, with Sarti left stranded by Chalmers' deflection of Murdoch's shot.

29. "So this is what all the fuss is about", thinks a young Celtic fan as he looks at the European Cup being grasped by Bobby Murdoch and Billy McNeill on the 'Welcome home' evening at Celtic Park, May 26th 1967. Bertie Auld (right) is the other Celt in the photo.

30. The Celtic squad and backroom staff show off the European Cup to the fans at Celtic Park on the 'Welcome home' evening at Celtic Park, May 26th 1967. A prominent figure on the right of the photo is physio Bob Rooney, who is wearing what appears to be a trilby or beach hat.

CHAPTER 10
Now's the day...

The somewhat chilly morning air could not dampen the sense of anticipation of what lay ahead some twelve hours later. A momentous event, the twelfth final of the European Cup no less, would soon stir them from their slumbers. Not only supporters of both finalists, but also more than 200 journalists (168 of them from outside Portugal) and representatives from 25 TV and radio stations and 83 photographers would assemble in the *Estádio Nacional* to cover a prestige fixture, which for the first time featured a British team, a Scottish side that had not previously met an Italian club in European competition. That club would have the good fortune of having its Lisbon odyssey recorded in a documentary, titled *Celtic*, which had been commissioned at the behest of chairman Bob Kelly, who had approached the producer, James Gordon, to make a half-hour film telling the story of a Scottish institution from its foundation.

However, Gordon's remit had expanded as the team had gone from success to success over the latter few months of the season, culminating in its appearance in the European Cup final, described by Gordon as "the happy ending to the fairy story." Permission to film the final, apparently the first shooting in colour of an event (for TV, cinema or documentary) which was still being transmitted in black and white for the Eurovision television network, had only been granted by the appropriate authorities as late as midnight on the night before the final. A four-man film crew would capture every move of the match before the footage was edited for inclusion in a real tear-jerker of a documentary. Remarkably, the same number of cameras was used by Portuguese TV, the host station responsible for providing live European-wide coverage, and Gordon's crew had the benefit of a superior vantage point, judging by the footage. (Modern, greatly enhanced coverage of a Champions League final would necessitate at least twenty cameras).

The positioning of the host's TV cameras would be criticised by *L'Equipe* as being "so high up as to make the play almost distant" a situation not helped by a stadium that had been designed for a dual role, football and athletics (with a running track around the pitch), glaring sunlight which was tough on the eyes of the commentators, and by the strip worn by the Celtic players. Brian Moore, later of ITV fame, stated years later that "more than a dash of guesswork" went into his commentary of the final for BBC radio's Home Service due to the Celtic players not having numbers on the back of their shirts, and the numbers on their pants being so modest in size as to require the eyes of a hawk to decipher, a problem which the non-Scottish occupants of the specially erected press stand also found a problem, resulting in widespread misidentification of players in the cases of several incidents in the final, notably in respect of Inter's early penalty award and Celtic's winning goal. Moore's unfamiliarity with the Celtic eleven and their unique strip, plus the fact that he had just flown out with his co-commentator Alan Clarke on the morning of the match (a BBC arrangement made "to keep the costs down", said Moore) would lead to the embarrassment of him crediting Bobby Murdoch with the winning goal, only for him to be corrected by the Scottish presence in their commentary booth (David Francey). Archie Macpherson, on his first foreign assignment for the BBC, was just as scathing when he told co-author Pat Woods about the inadequacy of the broadcasting facilities. Employed as a summariser, seated beside BBC TV's chief commentator Kenneth Wolstenholme in a small, tight cubicle topped by a little roof, he recalls the problem caused by the glare of the sun and "To make matters worse, they had installed a bench facing us on which was placed a bulky monitor (a TV set, really), and so it was like looking at the pitch through a letterbox."

The written press, initially at least, fared no better. George Aitken, formerly of Glasgow's *Evening Citizen*, recalled in an April 1976 *Celtic View* article that "the entire telephone circuit in the Lisbon stadium folded up before the match started." The *Scottish Daily Express*'s resourceful three-man team (John Mackenzie, Jim Rodger and Jimmy Sanderson) rushed down to the press room in the specially-erected stand and commandeered a Telex machine: while one reporter wrote a 'running' match report, a second acted as a messenger between the press box above and the Telex machine, where the third transmitted the copy back to Glasgow. Nearly a decade later, Mackenzie could not refrain from remarking sardonically that "The telephone which cost the *Scottish Daily Express* £30 has still to ring."

Equally bizarre was the decision of the *Glasgow Herald* not to send its football correspondent, Raymond Jacobs, to cover the most important match in the history of Scottish football, resulting in Gair Henderson, the chief football writer of its sister paper, the *Evening Times*, having to cover the event for both newspapers, necessitating an adjustment in style of writing (under the byline of 'A special correspondent') to accommodate the more august *Herald.* Jacobs briefly considered resignation, later denying to Harry Reid, a fellow journalist, that his absence was a product of a suspected anti-Catholic outlook on the part of the *Herald,* suggesting instead that it was a reflection of "the paper's Olympian disdain for professional sport in general and football in particular."

Such issues would have been but a sideshow for the Celtic hordes now pouring into Lisbon and putting Portela airport under unprecedented strain on the morning and afternoon of May 25th, when it had to cope with the bulk of 50 chartered flights. The sheer scale of it ensured that a day never to be forgotten would have its frustration as well as excitement. Gordon Cowan, a thirteen-year old schoolboy from the old Gorbals, which was then a Celtic stronghold in the days before redevelopment, recalled in the *Celtic View* of February 4th 2015 the fraught trip in the company of his two brothers and his father, arranged by their supporters club, the Sarsfield C.S.C., whose bus left from *The Tavern* pub at the corner of Florence Street and Ballater Street. In common with many of those who flew out that day, the feast of Corpus Christi (a Catholic holy day of obligation) the members attended mass, in their case at Lourdes Church in Cardonald, which was closer to Glasgow Airport, from where they were due to fly out at 09:15. However, soon after their arrival at the terminal building, they heard an announcement to the effect that their flight had been delayed for an unspecified period, leaving them to kick their heels as they watched their fellow supporters jet off, leaving the Sarsfield contingent as the only ones left at the airport. Eventually, a departure time of 12:30 p.m was announced, fans having been kept in the dark for the reason for the delay: their plane had made an additional journey that morning. Unsurprisingly, their wait on the tarmac to board the plane upon its arrival increasingly took on a level of desperation which was exacerbated by the sight of the Spanish flight crew sauntering to the plane. A four-hour flight left little time to get to the stadium for a 17:30 kick-off and, as the plane began its descent into Portela airport, the 'fasten seat belts' request went by the board. When the plane taxied to a halt and the doors were opened, the fans saw that there were no stairs by which to disembark and several of them decided to jump or "dreep" to the tarmac below and the planeload was soon stampeding through customs and airport control like "the migrating hoards of wildebeest of the Serengeti" before scrambling for transport, but it still meant that the Cowans arrived by taxi at the stadium only to learn that the score was already "Inter 1-0."

At least, after all the aggravation they were able to join the thousands of fellow fans who had gathered inside the stadium, the focal point of what had turned into a pilgrimage. For many it had been a case of scrimping and saving, working extra shifts, borrowing money from friends and relatives, and indeed turning their hand to anything to make sure they got there. The *Diário de Lisboa* instanced the entrepreneurship of one Alec Garland, who set up his own stall outside the stadium to sell Celtic rosettes in order to finance his trip and sold out his stock. The Celtic fans had already made an impression on the local populace and journalists (both local and foreign) as they turned Lisbon into a riot of noise and colour. The depiction by the correspondent of the Belgian *De Gazet Van Antwerpen* of boisterous supporters giving full vent to the love of their club underlined why the Portuguese took the Scots to heart in a big way. "From the early hours of the morning" said Marcel Geysen, "they wound their way through the city centre streets chanting favourite lyrics such as 'We shall not be moved' as they turned Lisbon into a green and white carnival. The locals looked on in astonishment as the visitors paraded through broad boulevards in the hours before kick-off, bedecked in Celtic colours – scarves, badges, top-hats, rosettes etc., many of them hand-made."

It was also clear that the Celtic contingent greatly out-numbered their Italian counterparts, who tried in vain to drown out the cries of "Celtic! Celtic! Celtic!" Rodolfo Paganini of Rome's *L'Unità* estimated a margin of 7:1 in favour of the Scots in terms of the number of supporters. Helenio Herrera had already anticipated the disparity in a *Scottish Daily Express* interview a few weeks earlier: "I think I will be lucky if there are 5,000 for Milan", adding that "the novelty of European Cup finals which is new to you [a put down of Celtic?] is wearing off for our supporters", though he must surely have also been aware of a loss of faith in the team on the part of the fans being a factor in the size of their support being dwarfed by that of Celtic's, whose ranks were swollen by their resourcefulness in acquiring briefs well in excess of their original allocation. The aforementioned, and perceptive, Inter fan Frank Arrighi, who flew to the match in a plane full mainly of supporters clad in green and white, noticed that his fellow Inter fans in Lisbon came mainly from the "well-to-do". He could not help but contrast that situation with the 1964 final, where 30,000 *Interisti* had been able to make the relatively short and inexpensive journey, mainly by bus, to Vienna.

Celtic fans, in contrast, had snapped up their allocation (and more), and Kevin Ewan of the *Glasgow Observer* and *Scottish Catholic Herald* caught their mood – and the broadening of horizons - perfectly in its June 2nd 1967 edition: "For Celtic, the European Cup Final in Lisbon was a million miles removed from an ordinary league game. Watching Celtic usually means a walk or a bus up the Gallowgate on a dreich Saturday afternoon or standing huddled at Parkhead on a winter's evening watching the rain or fog breaking through the floodlights' beam. Yet here they were these same supporters, 15-20,000 of them, sitting in the magnificent National Stadium and sipping iced beer. They came by boat and planes and trains, by car and on foot. They made up the friendliest and most welcomed invasion the ancient Portuguese capital has ever seen… everywhere the people of Lisbon made it quite clear what team they wanted to win. Even the police, forbidding at first sight with heavy rifles slung on their shoulders, gauged the happy mood perfectly." Equally perfectly, Ewan captured the whole wondrous experience in terms that only a Glaswegian of that era would have understood: "It was like a day doon the watter that ended on another planet."

For the finalists, however, it had now come down to what is called, in modern parlance, the business end of the season. It was not proving to be a comfortable experience for the men of Inter Milan. Jean Cornu of *L'Equipe* concluded from the taut expressions on view at the Italian camp ("Sarti is saying nothing, Picchi scowls") that "the Inter era" was ending. On the day after the match, the local *Record* newspaper published two photographs of players waiting at their Muxito hotel to set off for the stadium. The captions drew attention to how fed up they looked, a reflection no doubt on the resentment of having been cooped up there, and how worn-looking and forced were their smiles. There was no mistaking a depiction of unease in the Italian camp and the mood was not lightened on their arrival at the stadium to find their dressing room locked, denying them access for some twenty minutes and simultaneously providing an opportunity for more snaps of fed-up players.

Celtic's six-mile journey to the match venue could have been a nerve-inducing one, given the absence of the promised police escort contributing to the bus driver appearing to lose his way somewhat and becoming ensnared in heavy traffic heading for the stadium in one direction and for the beach in the other (it was a public holiday). However, the players whiled away the time by song and banter and, according to Steve Chalmers, "it was only when we approached the stadium that we encountered the crowds and the butterflies started to flutter in our stomachs." In fact, the belated arrival had the benefit of giving them little time to think about the final, having just enough time to have a look at the pitch and then get changed before kick-off. They were to find out that Inter had been allocated the so-called 'lucky' dressing room used by the Portuguese national side. Helenio Herrera had bagged it, contrary to the rules, during his visit to Lisbon the previous week. His team had used it for their training session the previous day. Celtic, on finding this out, had complained about the situation, resulting in a UEFA official telling a Portuguese newspaper that the dressing rooms allocation was, as per the rules, to be decided by a *sorteio* (a drawing of lots) at a meeting to be held by UEFA's executive committee on the morning of the final at the Hotel Estoril Sol in Cascais, some eight miles from the stadium. Inter duly won this minor skirmish, but it was to be their only victory that day.

By late afternoon, back in Glasgow, the city's streets were almost deserted. In its later editions, the *Evening Citizen* chronicled the sense of anticipation and the near frenzy surrounding the countdown: "For those hundreds of thousands of stay-at-home fans, in Glasgow and the millions throughout Britain, it was a case of get to the TV set or bust. Factories were allowing thousands of workers home early – or had sets specially installed – so that no one would miss the big game." The management of Fairfields shipyard had agreed to let workers off working overtime "in order to avoid mass absenteeism." The writer added "Pubs, restaurants and cafes – anywhere indeed with a television – expected to be crammed to the doors. Television rental firms in Glasgow were working at top speed throughout the day to keep on top of the demand for sets." Earlier that day, Gair Henderson of the rival *Evening Times* had found Jock Stein in reflective mood amidst the calm, relaxed atmosphere he detected in the Celtic camp. It was made clear to Henderson that the manager had impressed upon his players the expectations of Celtic fans everywhere, the city of Glasgow itself, Scotland, and the Portuguese, to whom he had promised on radio and TV that his team would attack and entertain: "This is the high point of Celtic history. We have every player fighting fit. They all know the responsibilities that rest on their shoulders and we are not going to be foolish enough to do anything that will jeopardise tonight", he told Henderson.

He may not have been aware of it, but until now the history of the European Cup had not been just a case of a Latin monopoly, but also essentially a tale of three cities – Madrid (Real: winners 1956 to 1960, 1966), Lisbon (Benfica: winners in 1961 and 1962), and Milan (A.C.: winners in 1963; and Inter, winners in 1964 and 1965). Now it was Glasgow's turn to attempt to join the elite, but the manager knew that he faced no easy task against a proud side that, whatever its recent shortcomings, contained no fewer than seven players set on winning their third winners' medal. Helenio Herrera, for his part, had been rather dismissive of his opponents in that morning's edition of the Zurich-based *Sports* newspaper, saying that "Celtic frighten opponents with their furious attacking play, but we intend to neutralize the hurricane", and his side's greater experience of the big occasion (an advantage Stein acknowledged publicly, and perhaps inwardly feared) was predicted by many to be a major factor in deciding the outcome. The heat, too, appears to have been a concern, judging by a local *Record* reporter present in the Celtic hotel after the team had partaken of lunch and had a limbering-up session on the lawn before setting off for the final and who overheard Jock Stein - and some supporters milling around - expressing a desire for some rain. Three days earlier, the Lisbon daily *O Século* had published the results of a survey of 22 Portuguese football personalities (players, journalists, administrators and referees), of whom fifteen plumped for

Inter as winners of the final, while only six went for Celtic, with one abstention. This had all the makings, it seemed, of a David vs. Goliath contest, the same newspaper noting that Celtic fans arriving at the stadium were soon made aware that the locals "would be pleased to see the Scots tear a strip off the arrogant Milanese team."

But now the time for talking and speculation was over. It was a case of "Let battle commence."

CHAPTER 11
...And Now's the Hour ‡

The twelfth European Cup final, May 25th 1967, kick-off at 5.30 p.m. at the *Estádio Nacional*, Lisbon, located in the Oeiras district 10 miles from Lisbon city centre. 'Lisbon' has become the shorthand for the venue and, indeed, for the final itself.

<u>Attendance:</u> 45,000 (official attendance supplied to Pat Woods, co-author, by Hans Bangerter, Secretary General of UEFA, in a letter dated July 7th 1987).

<u>Celtic (4-2-4):</u> Simpson - Craig, McNeill (captain), Clark, Gemmell - Murdoch, Auld - Johnstone, Wallace, Chalmers, Lennox.

<u>Inter Milan (4-3-3):</u> Sarti - Burgnich, Guarneri, Picchi (captain), Facchetti - Bedin, Mazzola, Bicicli - Domenghini, Cappellini, Corso.

(Line-ups taken from the authoritative *L'Equipe*)

<u>Substitutes:</u> Season 1966-67 saw the introduction of substitutes in UEFA competitions, but initially only in case of an injury to a goalkeeper. Celtic's nominated substitute for the final was John Fallon, Inter's was Ferdinando Miniussi. Neither was called upon.

<u>Referee:</u> Kurt Tschenscher (Mannheim, West Germany)

<u>Linesmen:</u> Rudibert Jakobi and Rudolf Eisemann (both Heidelberg, West Germany).

---

‡ This chapter incorporates the recollections of co- author Pat Woods, a spectator at the final, and of the referee Kurt Tschenscher, who was interviewed by co-author David Frier in July 2014, shortly before his death.

"The atmosphere was weird and wonderful and wildly Celtic from the moment Jock Stein took his players onto the field to test the turf", said John Rafferty of *The Scotsman*, who added that the manager came round to the dressing room "obviously deeply moved to see the crowd out there and he said: 'They are all Celtic supporters, it is inspiring'." He drew on this sight of the overwhelming support for his team to stress to his players a sense of occasion in his final words as they left the dressing room to take the field. They ran along the lines of reminding them that they had to perform as if there were no tomorrow, that they had done something that no other British club had done in reaching the final and to remember the Celtic fans who had come so many miles to support them. He also reinforced his message that "we have not come all this way to lose."

The teams emerged from the dressing rooms situated around 200 yards from the field of play itself, crossed an open courtyard based on Portuguese rural tradition, incorporating some arches of vaguely Moorish design, then entered a fifty-yard long tunnel to climb a flight of steps before emerging into the sunlight at the top of the stairway, a means of taking the field unfamiliar to British spectators, but it was alleviated for the Celtic eleven by them breaking into a chorus of *The Celtic Song*, prompted by Bertie Auld, which startled the Italians who seemingly did not know what to make of these mad Scotsmen. Unfortunately, the man who had made this song into one of the most famous anthems in world football, Glen Daly, could not be in the stadium to witness the most important match in Celtic's history since he was duty bound to perform at Glasgow's Metropole theatre that evening. He was thus deprived of that real sense of privilege that was felt by his fellow supporters lucky enough to be in a stadium described as a "giant arena" by referee Tschenscher, who told co-author David Frier that he was taken aback by the sheer size of it and the oddity of one side of the ground being open. The sense of anticipation mixed with tension, the thrill the spectators experienced as the two teams crossed the running track and the semi-circular grass area behind the goal to the left of the presidential area (the *Tribuna da honra*) was truly spine-tingling, made all the more spectacular by the vivid contrasts in jerseys of the two teams – the black and blue stripes which had earned Inter the nickname *I Nerazzurri*, and the green and white hoops of Celtic - but also the realization that they were about to watch the most important match in Celtic's history, a contest for the most prestigious trophy in club football between an all-Scottish side and an all-Italian one (albeit the latter if only by necessity).

Bobby Lennox would recall that, as the teams emerged from the tunnel, "first the sunshine hit my face and then the place was just a mass of green and white", and John Clark thought the setting akin to that of a Hollywood film

(*Field of Dreams* comes to mind), the players coming out to find a stadium bathed in sunlight and bedecked in green and white with a flurry of flags, banners and scarves both reassuring and inspirational to a Celtic eleven which was making the club's debut on live Europe-wide television. It seemed as if Glasgow had decamped to Lisbon. Even before the teams reached the centre circle there was the amusing sight before kick-off of the diminutive Jimmy Johnstone trying to negotiate a jersey swap at time-up, in some form of sign language, with the baffled giant full-back of Inter, Giacinto Facchetti, but elsewhere a skirmish was taking place which was intended to lay down a marker. Jock Stein had instructed substitute goalkeeper John Fallon to take possession of the nearest bench, which he duly did, sitting there with two policemen standing behind who came in handy to deter Helenio Herrera and his cohorts from claiming the same bench, enabling Fallon to indicate "One up for us" when Jock Stein arrived on the scene. An exercise in mind games, you might say, but in fact it was the calculated first instalment of payback time for Jock Stein's treatment in Turin. The Italian club may have had all the glamour and prestige, but the Celtic manager was determined that his club (not least in the eyes of his players) should not be viewed as a doormat for Inter.

Rodger Baillie, then a *Sunday Mirror* columnist, has stated that "like Scottish regiments, who sang their way into battle, Celtic were ready to take on a foreign foe." However, they were initially on the back foot, as Inter's start to the final made nonsense of pre-match speculation that Herrera was intent on a defensive pattern designed to secure a replay in the hope that Suárez would be fit for such a match, two days later, for with only two minutes on the clock they earned a free kick for a foul on Mazzola at the left-hand edge of the Celtic penalty area. Mazzola, reported to be playing despite a recent bout of bronchitis, took the free-kick himself, forcing Ronnie Simpson to snatch the ball before it reached the head of the inrushing Facchetti. It seemed as if Inter, moving the ball around slickly, were intent on administering a couple of early knock-out blows on their opponents, for just a minute later Simpson was forced into action again, blocking a close-in Mazzola header with his thigh following astute build-up play by Cappellini and Corso. In his weekly column in Glasgow's *Evening Citizen* two days later, Billy McNeill said that "perhaps the only time in the game that Inter were likely to do it [i.e. score] was in the first fifteen minutes", and because of this he hinted that Celtic may have been a bit nervy during the opening exchanges: "We were wound up, it was our first final." Tommy Gemmell revealed a year or so later that it took him twenty minutes to get his second wind after being initially affected by the heat, which made his legs feel heavy. Even so, the opening goal of the match would come at a time when Celtic seemed to be asserting themselves, with Jimmy Johnstone setting the mood by obeying Stein's instructions to keep Inter on the hop and get the crowd on Celtic's side with his skill on the ball. Nicknamed by one Inter fan as *La Zanzara* ('The mosquito'), he so tormented Burgnich with his pace and dribbling that when, early on in the match, J. L. Manning, a noted writer for the *Daily Mail*, rather fatuously observed to Hugh McIlvanney of *The Observer* that the little redhead's style was "not very economical", he was met by the riposte that "You just keep your eye on that defender, he'll be calling for a taxi soon to get him out of here." That defender, Tarcisio Burgnich, who later dubbed his opponent 'Houdini', would have shared his colleague, Sandro Mazzola's assessment of the demoralisation being inflicted by Johnstone and his colleagues: "The pace of Johnstone and Lennox, Celtic's wide runners, put Burgnich and Facchetti under pressure, thus restricting Facchetti – often a match-winner for us with his superbly timed up-field sorties – to defensive duties. Armando Picchi, our captain, and Aristide Guarneri found themselves up against two centre-forwards (Chalmers and Wallace) instead of the one they were used to coping with. This was something that Herrera had not foreseen."

Steve Chalmers makes a crucial point when he draws attention to the fact that the Celtic strikers didn't feature much in most of Celtic's many scoring chances in the final, their role being instead to make diagonal runs designed to draw their man-markers with them and allow the full backs, Jim Craig and Tommy Gemmell, and midfielder Bobby Murdoch to move into the vacated spaces. Jock Stein had sent out a Celtic side designed to cede nothing to Inter in terms of resourcefulness, flexibility and inventiveness, to give his men the "extra push" that Doug Gardner's preview in *World Sports* regarded as essential: "The secret of Inter's success, I think, is that Herrera has built up a side which by some strange alchemy can make any opposition, whatever its style, look as if it is playing the game just the way Inter want it to go." Stein had sussed this out, and he had told Hugh McIlvanney before the final that "By the time they find out we've done something wrong, we'll be doing something else." Central to that approach was the manager's insistence that Celtic did not let Inter dictate the pace of the game and thus stifle Celtic's superior resources of speed and stamina, having noted that Continental sides were inclined to do their best, most potent work, spasmodically (in bursts), in contrast to the more 'all out' approach of British clubs. In an interview five years later, he said that he had modelled his planning on another sport: "We knew that Inter would try to dominate us with their superior technique and with their defensive power. That was why we forced them, with our speed and strength, to return the ball to us as if it was really a game of table tennis. We surprised them. At the end Helenio Herrera couldn't believe what he had seen and spoke about 'muscular football'. In reality we didn't invent 'muscular football', but against Inter it was our only hope. We could only break down their rhythm by running twice as much as them and not giving up on any ball. And that is what we did. At the end, in truth, the scoreline did not adequately reflect the qualities we displayed in order to achieve our triumph" (*AS Color,* May 30th 1972 – a supplement published by the Madrid sports daily *Diario AS*).

It was a stratagem that was looking to bear fruit for Celtic as Johnstone, leaving the Italian defenders standing like lamp posts as he darted around and about them, twice tested Inter's goalkeeper Giuliano Sarti, firstly when he swerved inside Bedin to fire in a low shot which was smothered, then with a header from a Lennox cross which was tipped over the bar by Sarti. However, from the resulting corner kick Inter's famed counter-attacking suddenly struck gold as they broke quickly to strike the first blow in the eighth minute with a classic illustration of how Herrera had refined the *catenaccio* system to such a level of effectiveness that it was compared to a machine uncoiling from defence like a giant spring to punish errors made (or gaps left) by unwary opponents as the Italian side counter-attacked. Cappellini, who had been moving from one side of the pitch to the other in the hope of latching on to through balls from Mazzola or Corso, was rewarded when the former's astute 'threaded' pass enabled him (Cappellini) to head into the penalty area, running towards goal on the right hand side before full-back Jim Craig tried to block his attempt to turn inside and prepare to shoot with his left foot, only for the Inter forward to hit the deck. It looked to most like a clear penalty, but there were those who believed that Cappellini had overrun the ball and run into, or across, the Celtic player before going down as if auditioning for an Oscar. The referee, Kurt Tschenscher, was reckoned by many observers to be about fifty yards behind the incident but claimed afterwards in the Italian newspaper *La Gazzetta dello Sport* that he had no doubts about awarding a penalty, adding that the linesman (Jakobi) on that side of the play had signaled his endorsement of the verdict. Mr. Tschenscher told David Frier that from his perspective it was clear that there had been a foul (*"Aus meiner Sicht war das ein Elfmeter"*). However, among those who described the award as very harsh was a notable pair sitting in the stadium, Alfredo di Stéfano and Ferenc Puskás no less, as well as Gino Palumbo of the Milan-based *Corriere della Sera,* who stated that "when Cappellini went down after Craig's clumsy challenge few [presumably a reference to colleagues in the press stand] thought that the maximum penalty would be exacted, particularly since the referee was so far away from the area of the pitch in which the incident took place and yet exhibited no doubt by immediately running to the penalty spot." Intriguingly, a well known former Scottish referee of the time, Jack Mowat, was quoted as saying that the award was correct, adding that "many Scottish referees would have taken the easy way out and given a non-scoring free kick."

Mazzola duly converted the award, sending Simpson the wrong way. A setback for Celtic, a real sickener for everyone connected with the club. A source of apprehension, too, given Inter's formidable reputation for taking a lead and then ensnaring opponents in their defensive web. John Clark is quoted as follows in a superb 1980 history of the competition (by John Motson and John Rowlinson): "When they scored so early, I thought, God Almighty, what chance have we got now. But the thing was, we were back in the game at once." Foreboding gave way to renewed optimism with a startling rapidity as Celtic adhered to Stein's instruction not to give the Italian players a moment's rest, a tactic which he had assured his players would allow their superior fitness and stamina to prevail. Billy McNeill, writing in his column in the Scottish edition of *The Sun* at the time of the 25th anniversary of the final, claimed that the penalty award was the best thing that could have happened to Celtic: "We were so brassed off and angry that we lost any nerves we might have had." His immediate opponent, Renato Cappellini, concurred, insisting that it contributed to his team's downfall, since it lulled them into a false sense of security: "We sat back thinking we could smother the contest, but we reckoned without the Scots, who played like men possessed and - with stamina to burn - pinned us back into our own half, shooting from all angles" (Milan-based magazine, *Intrepido*, June 1st 1967). The sheer ferocity of Celtic's response was heartening for their supporters, but disconcerting to the Italian side, who probably anticipated the Scots trying to 'play their way' back into the game, a reaction which would have suited the masters of defence. Instead the award turned into a poisoned chalice for Inter, who, fatally, thereafter surrendered the initiative as they struggled to dictate the pace of play in the face of Celtic's incomparable will to win, their rapid interchanging at speed and their combination play.

An indication of the pressure exerted by the Scots lies in the stark figures laid out by Pierre Lameignère, who revealed in *Miroir Sprint* that Tommy Gemmell had either centred/ crossed the ball or had a shot at goal on sixteen occasions during the match, while Bobby Murdoch (an appropriate bombardier, being a son of wartime munitions workers) did the same on thirteen occasions as Inter's enforced retreat left them with virtually no defensive duties. François Thébaud of *Miroir Football* dismissed the notion that Inter's defeat was down purely to exhaustion, a theory which he regarded as "confusing consequence with the cause", which he called the losers' means of excusing defeat. Effectively, he maintained, Celtic wore their opponents out: "When have we last seen such an offensive (from the 6th to the 90th minute), when have we last seen a goal set up by one full back and scored by the other?"

In truth, the Italian goal was turned into a shooting gallery, as Celtic poured forward relentlessly in line with Stein's instruction that Inter had to be attacked from all positions bar the central defenders and goalkeeper. As Jim Craig once observed, Stein told his players that they had to go at opponents from all sides and all quarters and, the full back added, in that respect the manager had exactly what he needed when he came back to Celtic Park: "He had great midfielders in Bertie Auld, Bobby Murdoch and Charlie Gallagher, with real pace in the shape of Bobby Lennox, Jimmy Johnstone and Steve Chalmers. John Clark held it all together at the back with Billy McNeill beside him. It must have been a dream when he realised that everything he was looking for was within that dressing room." Given the manager's theory that, if you have at least eight players in your team performing well on the day you were well on the way to winning any match, in a final where every Celtic player rose to the occasion it would prove to be an ultimately irresistible combination. Celtic were giving the lie to pre-match suggestions in the Italian press that they were little more than a team of runners, though even after acknowledging Celtic's victory in his *Il Giorno* match report as thoroughly merited, Gianni Brera – whose fraught relationship with Herrera perhaps led him to focus on Inter's failings rather than Celtic's merits - could not resist damning the Scots with faint praise, characterizing them as "an honest, lively and courageous group of players, but not a great team." The sheer fluency, variety and spontaneity of their play, the precision of their passing moves at speed, was in stark contrast to the tactical and psychological inhibition of their opponents. Here was a display which was nullifying one aspect of Herrera's mind games, namely his pre-match jibe that "Celtic can not play as well on a dry pitch in Lisbon as a soaking one in Glasgow."

And yet, the defiant Sarti gave a fair impression of invincibility as his colleagues seemed to be gradually losing their composure and equilibrium as they struggled to cope with wave after wave of attackers who were giving Inter no chance to settle into their normal rhythm while their defensive machine was run into confusion by Celtic's relentless industry, likened by the dismayed Inter fan Frank Arrighi to the "buzzing of wasps in a bottle." It had all the appearance of death by a thousand cuts, imposed on a team seemingly defending from memory by a team with a ferocious will to win which had enabled the midfield tandem of Bertie Auld and Bobby Murdoch (described by Mazzola as Celtic's most influential player and by the Italian sports daily *Stadio* as "the most persistent thorn in Inter's side") to take a firm grip of the flow of play and become the springboard for the attacking surges which heartened the legions of Celtic supporters whose role was adjudged by the Continental press to be crucial. This was noted, for example, by José Sampaio of the local *Diário de Notícias*, who marvelled at the noisy and sustained backing of the Celtic fans, particularly when their side was behind in the final: "At times we Latins think we know all about passionate support for our teams, then along came these 'Celts' to provide us with lessons in the art of driving a team to victory." By contrast, the Inter support was subdued throughout, as indeed had been the case even before kick-off, a reflection of the apprehension induced by their discouraging recent form. Everything seemed to be against Inter, reducing Helenio Herrera to shaking his fists at his players and leaping along the touchline like a man demented, a sight described by one observer as "shouting his team into panic stations." He was seen to be pleading regularly with arms outstretched, screeching "*Come mai?*" (roughly translated as Italian for "What the hell is happening?"). His frantic pleading for his team to retain possession was in contrast, albeit deceptive, to the Buddha-like impassivity of Jock Stein observed by Lisbon's *Record*. In fact Sean Fallon, Stein's assistant, stated that the anxiety was palpable throughout on the Celtic bench, and Jock Stein himself described the "nerve-wracking tension at that pinnacle of the game as higher than that at an Old Firm match."

Somehow, however, Inter held out to the interval thanks to Sarti, dubbed "the man of a thousand arms" by Milan's *Domenica della Sera,* playing the game of his life. A veritable human wall, he had thwarted Celtic from the outset and underlined his brilliance when he catapulted himself into a horizontal dive to brilliantly push Gemmell's ferocious, net-bound, left-foot volley around the post. It was reported by a French newspaper after the match that Gemmell had applauded a Sarti save from one of his thunderbolts and sought him out at the post-match banquet to congratulate him on his performance. The watching Joe McBride, a Celtic striker sidelined by injury but present in the stadium, said afterwards that he counted eight attempts at goal that, against any other keeper than Sarti, would certainly have found the net. Jock Stein himself claimed that, but for the latter's superlative goalkeeping the score-line would have been 6-1 in Celtic's favour, although it should be noted that some continental reports also referred to some waywardness in the Scots' shooting as a contributory factor to the narrow margin of victory.

By contrast, Ronnie Simpson was a virtual spectator throughout, causing Spanish sports daily *Marca* to withhold a marking for him in its match report, though as half-time loomed he was called upon to deal with a tricky situation after a long Guarneri clearance downfield caught Celtic exposed at the back. Simpson came thirty yards out of his goal to deal with the threat, but quickly became aware that Domenghini was chasing him down in hope of exploiting a rare opportunity. The veteran keeper, however was sufficiently alert to not attempt to kick the ball clear at the risk of the Italian succeeding in charging down the ball and netting a goal which would probably have destroyed Celtic's hopes of a victory, Simpson opting instead to hold the ball at his feet before back-heeling it across the pitch to John Clark. Nonchalant though it seemed, it was an incident that strained the nerves of the Celtic bench, not to mention the players and fans. Three days later Simpson told the *Scottish Sunday Express* that Jock Stein was "dead right" to tell him that he came out too soon, for "that's why I got myself in a fankle."

It had been a heart-stopping moment, but one quite in keeping with an engrossing contest. The Inter players left the pitch at half-time to booing from the crowd for their negative performance, not only from Celtic supporters but also from Portuguese spectators, who had made no secret of their partiality for the Scots, their warm applause for Celtic's positive approach and the fervour of their fans being augmented by many of the locals viewing the Glasgow club as potential 'proxy' winners out of anger at the Italians' treatment of Benfica before the final two years earlier. Some Celtic players gave the referee 'stick' for the penalty award as they headed for the dressing room, being joined in their anger by Jock Stein, who was reported to have been overheard by an Inter official, Dottore (Dr.) Chiesa, a *consigliere* (advisor) to the club who spent the match beside Herrera on the bench, as saying to a startled referee that "Inter had placed an order for that penalty". The German football newspaper *Fussball-Sport* said, to no avail, that it was a matter that should be investigated by UEFA. Herr Tschenscher's denial to David Frier that he had been insulted by Stein can probably be best construed as a diplomatic response, given that Celtic's substitute keeper John Fallon was also a witness to Stein's tirade. The Celtic manager then turned his attention to Helenio Herrera as they both headed for the tunnel, fulminating against the tactics, most notably time-wasting, employed by the Italians in the first half. In the tunnel itself, according to the local *Record,* an angry Inter coach "made an offensive gesture towards Stein, leading to the latter grabbing Herrera by a jacket lapel", with only the intervention of Sarti (according to the testimony of an unnamed photographer in a different newspaper report) preventing the two coming to blows in the dressing rooms area. Certainly, Herrera had tried to put pressure on the referee before the final by telling the German newspaper *Bildzeitung* that "Herr Tschenscher should be aware of the Scots' ruggedness and be confident enough to blow his whistle in the opening 15 minutes or so", and Stein's apparent 'paranoia' may have arisen from reports emanating from Italy of Inter's influence on referees in Serie 'A'. Victory, however, has a soothing effect, for Stein was pictured in a Portuguese newspaper with the referee and his linesmen at Portela airport the following afternoon, looking for all the world as if nothing untoward had occurred the previous day.

Indeed, Stein had calmed down by the time he entered the Celtic dressing room, where he proceeded to tell his players to forget what had happened in the first half, since they could do nothing about it and it was more important to focus on the next 45 minutes. Reassurance was given of eventual triumph if they continued to play as well as they had been doing, the only caveat being that they were playing the ball too much into the heart of the Italian defence whereas it needed to be cut back more acutely across the penalty box. One of those absorbing this advice, Tommy Gemmell, also took the opportunity, like other team-mates to don a completely fresh strip in the shower, but he also put on rubber-studded boots instead of the leather ones which had been hurting his feet during the first-half. It was a change which, like Stein's advice, may just have been prescient, and if the occupants of the Celtic dressing room had had a spy in their opponents' dressing room they would have taken heart from the tension and disorientation that reigned therein, with Inter players drained of self-belief and some feeling the effects of the heat. Stein was to claim afterwards that the referee had to ask Inter four times to come out for the second half, and when they did emerge (with Celtic already kept waiting on the pitch) they - and the referee - were booed again. During the interval, a light aircraft had flown over the stadium, trailing a streamer advertising a bullfight at nearby Cascais three days later. It could be viewed as a metaphor for the final itself, but it was a contest with a debatable outcome given the stubborn nature of the Inter beast. Brian James of the *Daily Mail*, for one, was not sure of a happy ending for Celtic in a match which had taken on the aspect for spectators and TV viewers of a Goodies vs. Baddies affair. Taking stock of the state of play for his match report, he spoke for many when he wondered whether Celtic, who had done so much, could do any more. Inter, he said, playing with a calm that neither the situation nor their own slack marking and passing seemed to justify, were "holding what they had been given with a despicable repertoire of time wasting and temper-fraying tactics", including Sarti's ploy of delegating goalkicks to a colleague.

Immediately on the resumption, Celtic delivered a quick response to the doubters. During a goal-mouth melee, Burgnich performed a hitch-kick which almost beheaded Willie Wallace, but the referee rejected Celtic's penalty claims, opting instead to award an indirect free-kick. Gemmell's low shot was deflected past Sarti by Picchi and looked net-bound until the keeper did a back-flip again to grab the ball. The Celtic players claimed the ball had crossed the line, but the referee endorsed his linesman's signal to the contrary. It was a save that bordered on the miraculous, the fore-runner of many in a second half during which Inter gave up any pretence of being an attacking force as they were forced deeper and deeper towards their own goal to the backdrop of a crowd, particularly the Portuguese contingent, venting their fury at Inter's delaying tactics. Mario Corso, singled out as *the* symbol of Inter's impotence, being categorised as "a depressing sight, a veritable representation of a marble statue", was described by Frank Arrighi as "wandering about like a lost soul" as he was brushed aside by the rampaging Bobby Murdoch, a tireless and redoubtable midfielder playing with a right ankle that had been damaged early in his Celtic career and never properly healed, requiring it to be put in plaster before every match. So crucial was he to the team that he played through the pain barrier. "The Celtic line-up in the great years of the Stein era was Bobby first, then the other ten of us were slotted in beside him", said Billy McNeill in a tribute paid after Murdoch's death in May 2001. Mauro Bicicli, Suárez's replacement, was another conspicuous failure for Inter, a player who had been damned beforehand with faint praise as "a worthy schemer" being deemed anonymous throughout. Partly chosen for his defensive qualities, he had to suffer the ignominy of being dismissed in the Italian press's post-mortems as "an intruder into a great team" and having to endure a cruel quip about his surname when one writer said he should have been taking part in the *Giro d'Italia* cycling race rather than an important football match.

However, for all of Inter's failings, around the hour mark there were certainly Celtic players who were wondering if their dream would come true for all that their ceaseless determined onslaughts on Inter's goal resembled an unstoppable steamroller. Billy McNeill admitted in the match programme for the 2009 Champions League final that there were moments during that 1967 final when he thought that it was not going to be Celtic's day, that "we're going home with nothing." For his part, Tommy Gemmell told the *Scottish Daily Express* post-match that "the minutes were ticking away and it was beginning to look as if we were never going to score." Tommy Gallacher, writing in the *Weekly News* a week later, certainly believed that the outcome was very much in the balance, stating that the tension was almost unbearable in the early part of the second half as "Sarti kept up his brilliance and it soon became a question of who would crack first, Celtic through utter frustration, or Inter Milan through fatigue."

These are comments in line with the impression of several observers, including the correspondent of the Aberdeen *Press and Journal*, who thought that Celtic looked to be losing their composure and a touch of despair seemed to be setting in as "their play had become accordingly slightly ragged." There is evidence for that assertion in a tackle on the hour mark committed by Tommy Gemmell on Bedin, by the culprit's own admission a blatant foul born out of frustration. Ironically, however, it seems to have acted like the lancing of a boil, for a few minutes later the same Celt dispelled growing fears of Inter defying justice and brought a huge sense of relief to his team-mates, the anxious supporters and - not least - the occupants of the Celtic bench, who had been wondering just when the breakthrough would come, as assistant manager Sean Fallon later recalled: "It was very warm, but I was shaking like a leaf." Tommy Gemmell's self-expressed 'now or never' moment took shape when full-back Jim Craig, moving up on the right to intercept a Murdoch pass before making a bee-line for the Inter goal, became aware of his partner Tommy Gemmell starting his run to his (Craig's) left. Craig was set on giving the impression to the Italian defenders that he was intent on moving in for a shot, but his real intention was to draw defenders towards him and make an opening for Gemmell. As the latter came running alongside him shouting "Cairney, Cairney" (Craig's nickname), Craig showed perfect timing and technique when squaring the ball to his team-mate, whose 20-yard rocket left Sarti helpless as it arrowed to the top-right hand corner of his net, causing the stadium to erupt, said one match report, "as if Eusébio himself had scored for Portugal." Sarti and a couple of Inter players made a half-hearted, futile claim for offside against two Celtic players who had been in the goalmouth as they watched the trajectory of the ball. Momentarily, Gemmell was stunned: "I looked and I thought it was in the net but I came forward and looked again, just to make sure." He had every reason to do so, for the Inter captain, Picchi, had come out to attempt a challenge just as Gemmell was lining up his shot but stopped a few yards from the scorer and turned his back on the play. As Gemmell himself wryly observed, "If that guy takes one more pace and he blocks the shot, then no-one has heard of me." More pointed perhaps was his remark in the following day's *Scottish Daily Mail* that "If that shot had not gone through the Italian defence, I was at the stage of packing it in – make no mistake, I was becoming very frustrated." He had, however, fulfilled Jock Stein's prediction that he would score in the final.

There was no stopping Celtic now, but Inter's lingering stubbornness prevented the Scots from quickly administering the knockout blow before the final went into extra time. The concrete wall had been breached but certainly Sarti was still intent on keeping his team in contention, no matter that it now looked a case of mission impossible. A few minutes after the equaliser, he tipped a blistering 20-yard Murdoch volley over the bar, a spectacular save soon followed by a rare lapse when he was deceived by a long, floating ball from Gemmell out on the left which hit the junction of post and crossbar before being scrambled to safety by a defender. As he made his way back downfield, Gemmell noted how exacerbated and desperate Herrera looked "as he was on the verge of being unseated as the maestro of European and World football." In truth, once Celtic had breached the dam the coach had been reduced to silent impotence. There was nothing he could do now to motivate players who, as *Tuttosport's* Renato Morino could see from his vantage point in the press stand, were "in extreme distress." Inter were now so overrun and deflated, said one observer, that at times they resembled a wounded animal seeking to be put out of its misery, while Herrera was by now reduced to sitting on the trackside bench "unusually calm and, with a detachment of a medical examiner, looking on at the wreckage of the team he had built, *La Grande Inter.*" He may well have noticed one little-reported and poignant sight, that of Domenghini falling over through exhaustion, with nobody near him. The dousing of the Inter players with water by an occupant of their bench was clearly having no effect in alleviating their desperate situation as the pressure exerted by a Celtic team buoyed by their breakthrough was becoming irresistible. The mental tiredness was also taking its toll and was probably a contributory factor to a lapse in concentration ten minutes from time which resulted in Celtic being refused a blatant penalty. Sarti and Guarneri got into a tangle on the left-hand edge of the penalty area, enabling Willie Wallace to nip in and take control of the ball, but, just as he was about to head towards the empty goal, Sarti grabbed his legs and held him down. The referee stated afterwards that "Sarti fell over a Celtic player's legs".

Inter were out on their feet, punch drunk, but still there was no guarantee for Celtic that a replay could be avoided. And comparatively few present in the stadium would have been aware of the fuller implications of Inter managing to hold out for a draw in a final which looked like stretching into extra time. There existed the barely-publicized potential scenario of a replay scheduled for two days later (Saturday May 27th), at the same venue and kick-off time, ending in extra time at the end of which, if the proceedings ended in a draw, the destination of the trophy would be decided by the toss of a coin (!). It was a UEFA rule that would not be changed until 1970, when the penalty shootout was introduced. Imagine, then, the immense relief when the winner came in the 85th minute. Looking back, it still has a touch of the unexpected about it, an almost dream-like quality. With characteristic understatement, Steve Chalmers described it as follows in the *News of the World* (Scottish edition) three days later: "From a Tommy Gemmell cut-back, Bobby Murdoch smashed in a shot which was just going wide. Instinctively, I stuck my foot out quickly to side-foot the ball into the net." The ever-modest Celt makes no mention of his intelligent running off the ball to get on the blind side of the Inter defence. Indeed he was one of the two "stand-outs" (along with Tommy Gemmell) singled out by Jean-Phillipe Rethacker of *L'Equipe*, who highlighted Chalmers's adeptness in his deep-lying centre forward role, citing his running power and capacity for playing on the shoulders of defenders as a constant menace to Inter.

The goal, as Chalmers himself acknowledged in an interview in March 2000, was a product of hard graft: "It was the sort of thing we practised in training all the time. Jock would have midfield players firing balls hard into the box and Bobby Lennox, Willie Wallace and I would be in close to knock them into the net. Jock also loved it when he got the chance to finish things off himself with his left peg. It was invaluable against Italians, who marked you so tightly when you played against them that you felt that if you went to the toilet at half-time, they would follow you in." Stevie said in that article that he couldn't remember much of what happened immediately afterwards as the stadium went wild in "boundless joy" and two ball-boys were seen celebrating within yards of a motionless Herrera, who knew that the game was finally up. However, on the team bus taking the Celtic players to the post-match banquet, Chalmers was told by teammates that tears had been streaming from his eyes and that he "came back up the field like a man in a trance." In all probability none of them was aware just how much of the fairytale ending to the match it had been for a veteran who had netted the most celebrated piece of finishing in Celtic's history. In his regular column for the Scottish edition of the *Sunday Mirror* of May 28th 1967, Jock Stein stated that Chalmers' selection had been in doubt: "There was one man in Prague [in the semi-final second-leg] who took more out of himself than almost any other player that I had ever seen. That was our lone raider, centre-forward Steve Chalmers. He was buffeted, he was kicked. And all the time he helped to take the strain off the defence. I thought the punishment in that match had affected his fitness for the rest of the season but I decided to gamble on him for Lisbon and I almost wept for joy when he justified it by scoring the winning goal."

It was now a question of ensuring that, improbable though it seemed, Inter did not get any opportunity to conjure up an equaliser in a breakaway as the match drew to a close. Nonetheless, Ronnie Simpson recalled that he (and surely many Celtic supporters present) felt a "small, niggling fear that they might be lucky enough to sneak away and snick one in." As the minutes ticked down to the final whistle, Jock Stein, who was pictured wearing dark sunglasses and raising five fingers to indicate to his players the time remaining after Chalmers's goal, kept looking thereafter at his watch and, as another, un-named, occupant of the Celtic bench later told Tommy Gemmell, was also seen with his head down drawing pictures on the sanded track at his feet.

And then came the signal for the cavalry charge...

Result: Celtic 2, Inter Milan 1.

CHAPTER 12
Wild, wild, wild...

A minute or so before the referee blew his final whistle, Jock Stein rose from the Celtic bench and made his way towards the tunnel, seemingly overcome with the triumph that was now so tantalisingly close. "It had all become too much for me", he told the *Daily Record*'s Ken Gallacher on the way. He would soon be caught up in what the *Scottish Daily Express* called "the great Catherine wheel of colour" and "yelling cauldron of noise" that was a pitch invasion by "the joy brigade" as hordes of Celtic fans careered onto the field of play, following the pattern set (said some) by the post-match scenes at Wembley Stadium some six weeks earlier after Scotland had defeated England, the world champions (3-2), and, ironically, denying their favourites of a scenario that had been chanted on the Parkhead terraces in the months leading up to the final, namely "We'll be running round Lisbon with the Cup." As the match ended, said the *Scottish Daily Mail*, "police were swept aside as thousands of fans leapt the moat like assault troops and the Celtic team disappeared under an avalanche of green and white scarves, tammies and flags." The Chief of the Public Security Police for Lisbon, General Fernando de Oliveira, had talked of readiness on the part of the authorities in the capital and surrounding areas to cope with the influx of supporters, even boasting that "We are calling in the crack police guard, the reputation of the Scots' exuberance has preceded them in Lisbon", but at the stadium the National Republican Guard were simply not geared – or perhaps not really inclined? - to cope with a tidal wave that followed the final whistle.

The supporters' joy was part of the occasion and was perfectly understandable, but the celebrations on the pitch, which lasted at least twenty minutes, undoubtedly got out of hand and, indeed, were a touch scary. John Rafferty, writing in *The Scotsman* two days later pointed out that Celtic players ran the risk of serious injury as they headed for the dressing room: "Little Jimmy Johnstone said he was terrified when a Portuguese youth caught him by the neck." This was a matter of genuine concern, since nearly three weeks earlier, in an incident unreported in Britain, and which should have set alarm bells ringing for those responsible for match security at the stadium, the famous Eusébio had kicked out at a fan, who then fainted, during a pitch invasion at Benfica's stadium after the home club had clinched their domestic title. At the end of the final, players' boots, jerseys and socks were lost to souvenir hunters who showed no scruples about manhandling players in their frantic desire to commemorate their presence at the event. One fan said "I got John Clark on my shoulders and hoisted him up on my shoulders, somebody else stripped the boots off him." Ronnie Simpson, apparently, was the only Celt to reach the dressing room with his full football kit intact, and that only after a tug-of-war for his jersey. The match ball itself was stolen by a Celtic fan who punched it out of the referee's grasp before running back into the crowd. Herr Tschenscher told David Frier that one of his linesmen was keen to try and get the ball back, but the latter was told *"Laß es laufen"* ('Let it go'). The referee was sufficiently content to have kept his whistle as a souvenir and to be so amused by the antics on the pitch as to tell a German newspaper that the Celtic fans kissing the turf reminded him of Muslims at prayer. One fan, 30 -year-old Frank Docherty from Airdrie, went one further, taking home a six-inch piece of turf from the centre spot.

Archie Macpherson, meanwhile, found his attempt to secure an interview with Jock Stein on behalf of BBC Television an impossible task. Such was the chaos that he got no closer than ten yards from a manager who detested encroachments onto the field of play and was angrily and forcibly trying to persuade the jubilant, swirling legions to go back from where they had come. The broadcaster, who almost lost the shirt off his back in the scrum, also noticed how upset Tommy Gemmell looked as he was being mobbed, his arms being tugged and pulled by people who seemed intent on acquiring the Inter Milan jersey he had acquired in a swap with Mazzola. Shortly after realizing that it was mission impossible, Macpherson was then asked by a Portuguese official to broadcast an appeal to clear the pitch in order to allow the trophy presentation to get under way, but the din rendered his words virtually inaudible.

John Rafferty of *The Scotsman* certainly had a point when he asserted that the Portuguese did not have enough experience of staging events of this magnitude, citing not only the post-match events at the stadium, but also the aforementioned "inadequate and chaotic" telephone arrangements for the media, plus the confusion and delays caused by traffic to the match becoming snarled up around the stadium: "some had deserted cars and buses and set out on the five mile walk to the stadium." Celtic chairman Bob Kelly shrugged off the news that his Burnside home had been burgled while he and his wife were in Lisbon and joined in the criticism of the organisation of the final, particularly the inadequacies of the stewarding arrangements before and during the pitch invasion and the earlier failings with regard to the problems the Celtic party had in getting seated before kick-off, but also the dearth of programme sellers, which resulted in many fans returning home without a priceless souvenir. Kelly said that he had raised his complaints with UEFA, but this seems to have been done on an informal basis. He did, however, take the opportunity to vent his feelings in the Scottish edition of *The Sun*, for whom he had written a column in the week leading up to the final and a few days thereafter: "We [the British] are the best organisers of the big football occasion. There were so many loose ends in Lisbon. I think UEFA must lay down standards for the final to the home association. If these cannot be guaranteed, that country should not get the final. Arrangements and facilities for two competing teams and officials must always be of paramount importance. In this case, I feel Celtic certainly took second place. There is a lot more than 90 minutes involved in making the European Cup final a fitting occasion" (May 27th 1967). There was a suggestion in Rafferty's article that Tom Reid, the President of the Scottish Football Association, and Fred Denovan, the Secretary of the Scottish League – both of them guests of Celtic FC at the match – would raise Kelly's concerns with UEFA, but, even if they did, it was to no avail, for at their meeting in Geneva six weeks later, UEFA made a unanimous declaration that the organisation in Lisbon had been "wonderful." Of course, in view of the earlier insistence from both the FPF and UEFA that this final had to be played in Lisbon (as will be revealed in a subsequent chapter), it would have been a considerable embarrassment to both organisations to draw any further attention to things which had gone wrong on the day.

None of which overshadowed the scenes both outside and inside the Celtic dressing room, which, said one observer, "vibrated like an earth tremor" during the post-match celebrations. An ecstatic Jock Stein had set the tone when, after battling his way through the hundreds of delirious fans, including a "gloriously drunk Glaswegian" who had unfurled a banner emblazoned with the unlikely proposal of "Jock Stein for Pope", he came down the tunnel leading from the pitch yelling to waiting supporters, "The greatest night of my life, of all our lives." That sheer delight and excitement, mingled with a hint of disbelief at the enormity of the achievement, was also in evidence when he joined his players who were crying with joy: "I can still hardly believe that all this is true", he said, "I can say only that no manager has ever been given so much by his players and to say that I am proud of them is a complete understatement of the case", he told one reporter, sentiments he underlined when, welling up as he looked at players weeping unashamedly, he grabbed another newspaper man by the shoulders to roar "What a result, what a performance!"

The football writer Tommy Gallacher was surprised to see the manager so overcome with emotion: "It's not often you see Jock like that", but the exultation was not only an expression of delight but also one of sheer relief, a release from tension and strain, as Stein hinted to the local *Record* when he told one of its writers that facing Inter had "caused him some sleepless nights". Speaking at the time of the 25th anniversary of that unforgettable day, the veteran goalkeeper Ronnie Simpson, who had experienced unbelievable success in the few years since joining Celtic in September 1964 was, understandably so in the circumstances, the player most deeply affected by it all. He surely spoke for all his colleagues when he revealed to the *Celtic View* the state of mind prevailing in that dressing room: "I'm not ashamed that I sat and cried in the dressing room after the game. It was just a spontaneous show of emotion as it began to sink in that we had become the first British team to win the European Cup. I shed tears of joy, relief, happiness – just about every emotion. It was all swirling around my head and was also a demonstration of how much it meant to me to play for the club." Bobby Murdoch, who had been weeping tears of joy from the moment of time-up until he reached the dressing room, was so overcome with emotion and exhaustion that he gave a garbled interview to a Portuguese radio reporter and wore his boots while taking a shower (although there may have also been a precautionary element to this given the prevalence of souvenir hunting).

The dressing room, situated as it was in an open courtyard close to the open side of the stadium and therefore relatively easy to access at will, was a veritable cauldron of noise as it was besieged by well-wishers, reporters of every variety (print, radio and TV) and several fans, many of them anxious not only to congratulate the winning side but also to acquire some keepsake of the occasion, a spate of ransacking in a supposed sanctuary which forced Tommy Gemmell to arrange for an acquaintance to stand guard over a locker containing the full-back's swapped Inter Milan jersey. The celebrations were so intense that an official, either from the Portuguese football federation or UEFA, sent to summon the Celtic captain to collect the trophy, was "shown the door" on three occasions before it was realised who he was. There then ensued the ludicrous spectacle of Billy McNeill, accompanied by assistant manager Sean Fallon and some helpers (including John Rafferty of *The Scotsman* and Hugh McIlvanney of the *Irish Independent* and *The Observer*), having to make his way across the pitch to the presentation rostrum. James Sanderson had said in that day's *Scottish Daily Express* that the winners would be asked to perform a lap of honour before being presented with the trophy, but it seems more likely that only the captain would have been able to gain access to the presentation area, given how crowded it was with dignitaries, not to mention the practice at the Portuguese national finals played in the stadium in that era for only the captains of both finalists to attend the handing over of the trophy.

Billy McNeill has confessed to having been "very scared" during the foot-by-foot progress through the cavorting Celtic fans which left his ribs, shoulders and arms reminding him for days afterwards of the friendly, if over-enthusiastic buffeting he had taken as a path was forced through the deliriously happy throng. He then had a steep climb up a stairway (120 stone steps, no less) to reach his destination. As he neared the top, his wife Liz was sufficiently alarmed by her husband's obvious exhaustion as to fret about the disastrous prospect of him toppling over – due to the lack of a safety rail – during the presentation ceremony on the *Tribuna de Honra*. Fortunately, there ensued what may well be the most iconic and most photographed presentation ceremony in sporting history, with images being captured from the section below the rostrum, both sides of it and from above (from atop the roof of the white colonnade behind the marble rostrum). In an era where Celtic teams were routinely dubbed "The Pope's eleven", there was an intriguing symmetry (or fate, the more theologically-inclined might say) in the fact of the trophy being handed over by Américo Tomás, the President of Portugal, who earlier that month had greeted his Holiness Pope Paul VI as the latter disembarked from his plane at Portela airport en route to visit the shrine of Fátima. Whatever, there was something truly majestic and spectacular about McNeill, now composed and looking dignified after his ordeal, holding the European Cup aloft "in a triumphant pose of a Greek god" (John Rafferty) or standing high "like an Olympic torchbearer, thrusting the silver trophy at the summer sky" (Ken Jones of the *Daily Mirror*). For the first (and only time to date, up to and including the 2016 event) the final had been won by a team playing in green.

The shambolic scenes leading up to the presentation must have prompted a realisation amongst officials of UEFA and the Portuguese Federation that McNeill and Fallon – for reasons of both personal safety and the security of the trophy – could not possibly go back the same way, and so a car was laid on to take them around the perimeter of the stadium to the Celtic dressing room, a journey which was interrupted by a number of policemen who wanted to have photographs taken with McNeill and the Cup, including General Raul de Castro, Commanding Officer of the National Republican Guard, no less. It is the only time in the history of the competition that such a precaution has been required, so that (while the spectacle offered on the pitch had been of the highest standard), it is hard to escape the conclusion that the open-plan design of the National Stadium itself contributed to the post-match chaos.

Before McNeill had left the dressing room there had been indications just how much that the match had taken out of the players both mentally and physically. There were reports in foreign newspapers of Tommy Gemmell having entered the dressing room suffering from cramp and of Steve Chalmers lying stretched out on a table. Now however, there were scenes of unrestrained joy as they caught their first sight of the prize which made their strivings, their aches and pains, all worthwhile. Hugh McIlvanney, reporting the post-match happenings for the *Irish Independent*, was a witness to the scenes in the spartan, cement-walled room to which Billy McNeill returned with the trophy: "Soon his team-mates, some of them weeping, all of them almost hysterical, were drinking champagne from the huge silver cup. The dressing room was a joyful bedlam, with players singing and cheering as loudly as the supporters who had barged their way in." "This is the greatest night ever, the greatest", shouted Bertie Auld. "What a performance", Stein kept muttering, "what a performance…" The real drama was, however, served up by a compatriot of the latter, another man raised in the West of Scotland coalfields. The journalist Rodger Baillie was a witness to a scene which has become the stuff of legend: "The door burst open with the ferocity of machine-gun fire, the figure framed in the entrance to the dressing room would have doubled as an FBI agent in a Hollywood gangster movie of the Thirties. But instead of James Cagney it was a man whose mannerisms in so many ways were a carbon copy of the legendary film star. The changing room hubbub suddenly stilled as Bill Shankly advanced towards Jock Stein and in that unique rasping voice boomed: 'John, you're immortal'." Typically, added Baillie, Shankly never referred to Stein as Jock, but always by the name his family used for him. George Aitken of Glasgow's *Evening Citizen* stated that the Liverpool manager followed this up by saying of Inter that "they are good technicians but they haven't got what the Scots have got", thumping the area of the heart with his fist to underline his point.

It is an episode that has passed into the folklore of Lisbon, but, oddly, Shankly gave two ill-judged interviews that same evening which seemed to take the gloss off Celtic's triumph, albeit one of the interviewers, Bernard Joy of London's *Evening Standard* said that the Liverpool manager did not want to minimise the Scottish club's feat. Shankly was quoted as telling him: "Let's be fair about it. Inter were only a shadow of the side of two years ago. Spurs, of our League clubs, would certainly beat them – probably more easily than Celtic did." Why Spurs is unclear – perhaps because they had won the F.A. Cup the previous Saturday, but in any case Shankly was clearly unaware that Celtic had beaten the London club twice and drawn once in their three clashes in North America the previous summer. He added to an element of almost sibling rivalry with his fellow countryman by telling David Miller of the *Sunday Telegraph* that "We [Liverpool] would have beaten Inter earlier on this form". His team's 1965 semi-final exit at the hands of Inter was still a source of considerable irritation to Shankly, who clearly believed that it had denied him the history-making honour achieved by Jock Stein.

Neither Stein nor Shankly, however, would have had any sympathy for Helenio Herrera in his hour of bitter defeat. The latter had headed straight up the pitch side at time-up, studiously averting his gaze from the celebrations of the Celtic fans. He proceeded to lock himself in the Inter dressing-room along with his players for a debriefing lasting 45 minutes or so, during which he turned a deaf ear to the pleas for access from the club doctor, Angiolino Quarenghi, and the President, Angelo Moratti. One of the waiting Italian journalists quipped that Herrera was frightened to come out: "They are cutting his throat", he said, a reference to critics who were already sharpening their knives. When the door was finally opened, said the Dutch journalist Ed van Opzeeland, the room resembled "a funeral parlour where the faded glory was laid out." There was an unmistakable sense of the end of an era, the inevitable outcome, said a Milan-based journalist to Doug Gardner of *World Sports*, of Inter being the foremost representatives of a domestic game sinking in a sea of *lire*: "The players are paid so much money that they are afraid to go all out in the Scottish style in case they get serious injury and lose their lovely and expensive living. So they take no chances. Herrera, who is paid more than anybody, doesn't want them to take chances in case they make mistakes and his lovely living disappears as well." Excuses for the defeat would trickle out in the years to come: food poisoning at the Muxito hotel, pre-kick off cold showers that left players feeling dizzy, scorching heat which turned the stadium into a furnace (as if Italy was not familiar with heat) and, most bizarrely of all, the wind (if anything, surely a light breeze) not favouring Inter in the second half.

Already the recriminations were under way. Moratti, the Inter president, gracious in defeat, was telling the press that Celtic were playing very well and deserved to win, but as he was in the process of adding that only two players, Sarti and Corso (his favourite player), had played up to their usual standard, his eldest son Gianmarco intervened to say, rather sarcastically, that Corso "wasn't even on the pitch." Back in Italy, where the sporting press was in meltdown over what was viewed as a humiliating defeat and an affront to national pride, the Turin-based *La Stampa* would carry a quote by AC Milan coach Arturo Silvestri which was akin to a dagger being slipped into their local rivals: "Only the Inter jerseys were on the field." When Herrera finally emerged from his seclusion, his claims that the absence of Suárez and Jaïr and the necessity of fielding a "half-fit" Mazzola had prevented a more positive outlook by his team, and that Inter would recover from the setback, were met with scepticism from Italian reporters whose uppermost thought was about the coach's future - they were already concluding that he was living on borrowed time. That verdict was confirmed by a defeat at Mantova seven days later, ironically the result of an error by Sarti, which cost Inter the *Scudetto*. Adding insult to injury, Sam Leitch of the *Sunday Mirror* reported that, shortly after the final whistle in Lisbon, a loudspeaker outside the Inter dressing-room had blared out Sandy Shaw's recent Eurovision Song Contest hit *Puppet on a String*, perhaps a piece of mischief on the part of a stadium employee with an antipathy towards the Milanese side? Whatever, Leitch regarded it as splendidly appropriate for "Herrera's tired, outmanoeuvred and bewildered Italian footballers - puppets one and all!"

Jim Craig has attested to the huffiness of Herrera and, by way of contrast, to the sportsmanship of the defeated Inter players, who, as Celtic left the stadium to head to the post-match banquet, "lined up and applauded us". Allan Herron of the *Sunday Mail* described the exhilarating and emotional bus journey into the city of Lisbon itself: "My fellow passengers are the human tornadoes of Celtic. Masters of Europe they had become. Boys now men. Scotsmen with the aura of greatness once possessed by Real Madrid, Benfica and Inter. IT HASN'T SUNK IN YET. We journeyed through an avenue of madness. Or so it seemed. Men wrapped in green and white. They roared and waved at the bus. They ran after it. Some had no shirts, some had no shoes. Hundreds wept in the sheer ecstasy of it all. Blistered by the sun. Drained of their strength by the greatest football occasion they will ever see in their lives. THESE WERE THE MEN WHO MEANT SO MUCH TO CELTIC. THE FANS. Many of them had spent their last copper to cheer 'The Bhoys' in Lisbon. Many hadn't a clue how they'd get home again. They may never see the wife again! But what the hell do we care now! Celtic had won. And we were here to see it". When the bus pulled up to a small square in the Alfama district, an old part of Lisbon overlooking the Tagus estuary, the passengers walked up the narrow, cobbled Rua do Chanceler into the prestigious *Varanda do Chanceler* restaurant. Jock Stein and his assistant Sean Fallon carried the blue case with golden handles which contained the European Cup into the restaurant, flanked by a guard of honour of clapping local people, a continuation of the applause directed towards the bus by the citizenry of Lisbon from kerbsides and windows as it sneaked its way through the streets.

Inter were at least an hour late in arriving at the banquet, the result of both Herrera's lock-in and the fact that, having journeyed to the match in their tracksuits, they had to return to their hotel to get changed. The Celtic party applauded the Italians all the way from the restaurant door to their tables, but the Inter party looked very downcast ("like affronted grandees", said one French journalist), giving the impression that they would rather be anywhere else. The banquet itself was rather chaotic, the food supply and service being rather erratic, the din created by the babble of voices being such that at one

WE'LL ALWAYS HAVE LISBON

stage, the Celtic chairman, Bob Kelly, threatened to sit down if those present didn't shut up during his speech, but nothing could spoil the day for one group, as John Mackenzie of the *Scottish Daily Express* noted: "Dazed Celtic players prattled on, eyes as bright and sparkling as the champagne they drank. They still didn't believe it." It was understandable that Herrera's players would be subdued, but it was noted that Jock Stein was ill at ease, as if the tension and the strain of preparation had drained him of the joy and satisfaction that he should have taken in a great personal triumph, an anti-climactic mood that overtook him more than once in his career. The BBC broadcaster Archie Macpherson was present at the banquet and told co-author Pat Woods that the manager seemed more intent on keeping a beady eye on the conduct of his players, a perennial preoccupation of his, and he also had the impression that Stein was struggling to come to terms with the magnitude of his personal achievement: "At no stage did Jock Stein seem to be enjoying himself." That perception is reinforced by the fact that at one stage he rebuked an UEFA official whom he had overheard seeming to belittle Celtic's victory by expressing his sympathy for Inter having to cope without Suárez and Jaïr. Stein's vehement contradiction of the official's viewpoint took the latter aback. To nobody's surprise, no words were exchanged between Stein and Herrera, who was said to have looked bitter and surly during the banquet. They sat at opposite corners of the room, and one reporter observed of Herrera's discomfort that "you could see his eyes wandering towards the European Cup in which Stein's grinning face was reflected." Stein himself was still smarting from the snub that Herrera had delivered to him not only at the banquet but also after the final whistle, stating cryptically that "he must have been the only person in Portugal not to congratulate me."

Elsewhere in the city, Celtic fans had taken over the streets, bringing smiles to the faces of the astonished *lisboetas* as they emerged from special trains, motorcars and buses, singing and cheering, brandishing and waving vigorously their banners and flags as if, in the words of one Lisbon daily, "they had reached their promised land." John Quinn, reporting from Lisbon for Glasgow's *Evening Times*, said that for eight hours after the final Celtic supporters "turned the city centre into a green and white paradise of song" and that thousands had gathered in the main square in its heart - Praça Dom Pedro IV (popularly known as the Rossio) - to watch the fans "going through their full repertoire of songs and dances." The *Greenock Telegraph*, in its coverage of the trip made to the final by the local Celtic supporters' club, noted that bars, cafes and nightclubs in the city centre were the scenes of wild celebrations into the early hours of the morning. "Lisbon belonged to Glasgow", the report added, instancing how Celtic fans "climbed street signs to loud chants of 'Cel-tic, Cel-tic' while local policemen looked on in amazement." Typing out his thoughts on the match late on in the evening against this background of deafening revelry, Roberto Figueiredo da Vaz, a correspondent for the Barcelona sports daily *Dicen*, was moved to observe that the Celtic fans had brought "a colourful note to the game of football the likes of which has rarely been seen." Towards midnight, there were frantic efforts to round up fans and get them to Portela airport to catch flights that were departing at regular intervals. When members of the trip organised for regulars of the *Kimberley Queen* (Tollcross) bar and three other Glasgow East End supporters' clubs turned up for a scheduled 11.30 return flight, they found the number of planes to be so large that many were even parked on the grass verges. Indeed, such was the general state of confusion that one pilot was quoted as saying that group arrangements had to be scrapped and that the aircraft were just filled up with passengers on a first-come, first-served basis. None of which fazed one young boy, a sleepy-eyed Celtic fan noticed by the Belgian journalist Marcel Geysen couching in the airport lounge, "his face still glowing with pride at the memory of the 'invincible' Inter Milan being overcome by his favourite team." In the words of a noted song, sweet dreams are made of this.

CHAPTER 13

"Paradise in Kerrydale Street"

And now it was time to go home for the majority who had revelled in the experience of a lifetime, one which was made all the more memorable for Glasgow's *Evening Times* reporter John Quinn (covering the 'Celticade' of cars which had left Glasgow four days before the final) by a touching final reminder of the impact on the Portuguese capital of the invasion of those high-spirited people from the north: "One moment of worry remained for me as I was driving away from Lisbon. A car tailed me for miles, flashing its lights non-stop. Eventually, I pulled over and the other driver leapt out. Thinking the worst, I prepared for trouble only to find the driver presenting me with a bottle of their vintage port to celebrate Celtic's triumph."

The Celtic fans who remained in the city were clearly in no mood for the party to end. Indeed they would have celebrated into eternity. The *Liverpool Echo* reported on their determination to prolong the moment with a wave of enthusiasm such as even the football-crazy city of Lisbon had never seen: "Glasgow Celtic fans created huge traffic jams through Lisbon streets today, still celebrating last night's European Cup victory after a night of revelry. The jubilant Scots brought chaos to rush hour traffic when they paraded through central Lisbon carrying flags and banners and shouting their war-cry 'Celtic, Celtic'. A senior Lisbon Police Officer said 'We turned a blind eye in the special circumstances.'" At the same time, a number of their fellow supporters (estimated at between 100 and 250) had begun turning up at the British Embassy seeking financial help or replacement passports to get back home. One fan at least had no such worries, being in a position to offer Anne Deas, Tommy Gemmell's fiancée, the sum of £500 - a lot of money then - for her thirteen-guinea green and white hooped coat. She refused, prompting Jock Stein to tell her that she was mad not to accept.

That same morning, the Celtic party was still coming to terms with the enormity of the club's achievement. When Jock Stein moved off to join his players around the hotel swimming pool shortly after giving a newspaper interview, he was overheard muttering "We really did it... we really did it." That sense of disbelief still lingered as they were applauded all the way from their hotel as the bus made its way that afternoon to the airport for the journey home. When their chartered Dan-Air Comet plane touched down at Glasgow Airport, around 6:45 that evening, there to greet them on the tarmac were John Johnston, the Lord Provost of Glasgow, Peter Scott (the vice-President of the SFA, the chairman, Tom Reid, being a guest of Celtic in Lisbon) and John Lawrence (Chairman of Rangers FC). Bob Kelly, the Celtic chairman, "beamed with delight", said one newspaper, "as he appreciated the gesture of Glasgow's civic chief and the boss of their greatest rivals."

John Lawrence had readily accepted the Lord Provost's invitation to accompany him to the airport. He had been in London on business the previous day, he told Glasgow's *Evening Times*, but there were no facilities in the airport to watch the final and so he had to book a room in a hotel to watch it. Celtic's performance, he said, had been "truly magnificent, and they thoroughly deserved to win the Cup." His magnanimity was shared by his club's manager, Scot Symon, who had forecast a Celtic victory in the Italian newspaper *Tuttosport*, telling his interviewer that "I shall be a Celtic fan on Thursday", following that up after the final whistle with a congratulatory telegram to Jock Stein and telling the *Scottish Daily Express* that "Words fail me, it was a football performance out of this world." Relationships at board level between the two rival clubs had a greater level of mutual respect then. In the 1950s, Bob Kelly himself had been the beneficiary of Rangers support in his successful candidature for the post of vice-President (and later President) of the SFA.

One can understand the appeal by officials and police for Celtic fans to stay away from the airport stemming, apparently, from a desire to avoid a 'massing' similar to that in 1962 when Rangers had returned unbeaten from a Russian tour to find an estimated 10,000 supporters crowding their aircraft as it came to a stop on the tarmac, overwhelming the police presence as they swarmed over the runway. The usual airport formalities having been kept to a minimum, the Celtic team bus - with the gigantic European Cup on display at the front - set off with an escort of police motorcycle outriders on its twelve-mile drive to Celtic Park. It was followed by a cavalcade of motorcars occupied by fans who had shunned the wishes of officialdom in their determination to join in what one newspaper described as "the motorcade of joy." Out it swept through Renfrew, then along Shieldhall Road, through the Clyde Tunnel onto Dumbarton Road, then along Argyle Street, through Glasgow Cross and on to the Gallowgate before turning down Springfield Road, then right into London Road, the final leg of a journey during which, said a *Daily Record* reporter, it had been "deafening in the streets as thousands of car horns blared a victory fanfare when the cavalcade sped past." Crowds lining the streets, not solely Celtic fans, had cheered themselves hoarse as they joined in the acclamation. "Women and children leaned from tenement windows waving flags and banners", said the *Courier and Advertiser* (Dundee), "and men dashed from pubs raising glasses of whisky and beer in far from silent tribute: the window banners proclaimed 'Celtic are the greatest' and 'Welcome the Bhoys home' and some daredevils even bellowed their welcome from precarious places on the tenement roofs."

The last lap of the return home could be likened to a journey through the club's birthplace and indeed its past, taking the form of a heritage trail as much as an embrace by a community which had long associations with the new European champions. The celebrations were to have echoes of what *Scottish Referee* had called the "perfect turmoil" and "hearty rejoicings" ("Bands, you ought to have seen them") which had abounded during the East End's reaction to "our team" Celtic's first major triumph, their Scottish Cup final victory over Queen's Park in April 1892. From the moment the bus passed through the Trongate into the Gallowgate, the jubilation in the solidly working-class Calton district had a special tinge. In his report for *The Times* (London), Hugh Cochrane caught its flavour: "The full repertoire of Celtic songs pealed prodigiously through the tenement streets, the banshee cry of C-E-L-T-I-C swelled from the wet mouths of the faithful with an eerie rapturousness, and old men at the kerbside talked fumbling comparisons of the glorious days of Patsy Gallacher, Jimmy Quinn and John Thomson, the martyr goalkeeper."

The proud driver, Dan Donaldson, a Calton man from Bain Street, would have been well acquainted with the 'Celtic' territory through which the bus passed: firstly, Kent Street (adjacent to Glasgow Cross), which gave its name to a supporters club (the Kent Star CSC) which had fans, including the young Terry Dick (son of the well-known entertainer Glen Daly), who volunteered during the 1960s to clear the terracings of Celtic Park of rubbish on the days after matches for the reward of a ten-shilling note, a bottle of Whitbread ale and a glass of whisky. Nearby, facing the Barrowlands ballroom and 'Barras' market in that same decade, was Glasgow Jazz Club Promotions Ltd., a shop run by a peppery London-born Marxist called Clifford Stanton, who claimed to be a rights owner of Catholic hymns and who sold 'Irish rebel' records as a lucrative sideline, but in whose establishment, during a meeting with the aforementioned Glen Daly (real name: Bartholomew Francis McGovern McCann Dick, better known as 'Bartley'), was born the idea of Glen recording *The Celtic Song,* one of the most celebrated anthems in world football.

A few hundred yards further on, close to the old Meat Market was Dunlop's the butchers, who supplied, as they had done for the European Cup-Winners' Cup second leg against Dynamo Kiev the previous year, the huge parcel of meat, poultry, loaves, tomatoes, etc., which Celtic took to Lisbon to make the players feel at home (a penny for the thoughts of the head chef at the Palácio hotel!). Up came the junction of the Gallowgate with Bellgrove Street and Abercromby Street, where in the early evening of September 5th 1931 the young 'Bartley' Dick saw - in the words of his son Terry - "groups of men, and women with babies in shawls, gathering at street corners and pub doors waiting anxiously for news in the 'extra' editions of the Saturday newspapers of the young Celtic goalkeeper, their 'darling Johnny' Thomson, word of whose serious (fatal) injury at Ibrox Park that afternoon had quickly spread. Their concern had a personal touch, for they had known him when he was in digs in the Gallowgate (at its intersection with Cubie Street), as a regular visitor in the company of Celtic manager Willie Maley and the soon-to-be legendary centre forward Jimmy McGrory to the St. Mary's parochial hall", the same St. Mary's in Abercromy Street which had given birth to Celtic in November 1887 in a "mean little church hall" off the adjacent East Rose Street, now Forbes Street.

As it made its way a couple of hundred yards along the East End's main thoroughfare, the single-decker came parallel with Slatefield Street, where in the 1890s Tom Maley, one of Celtic's most famous and popular early players, lived up to the new club's charitable ideals in his capacity as superintendent of an industrial school where orphaned and homeless boys were provided with elementary education, remedial care and meals while they learned useful skills. Close by, at the corner of the Gallowgate and Whitevale Street, there had been a little cobbler's shop where, for nearly half a century (up to around 1960), the boots of the Celtic players were repaired by the Diamond family. In a May 1958 interview for the *Glasgow Eastern Standard,* Frank Diamond Sr. could recall the days in the early part of the century when the boots were brought to the shop in a spring-cart drawn by a horse on loan from Dalbeth Cemetery, two miles east of Celtic Park: a horse, incidentally, which was also used to roll the pitch at the stadium. From the days of Jimmy Quinn right through to Bobby Evans in the 1950s, said Mr. Diamond, "hundreds of little boys crowded the shop on these occasions [the delivery of the footwear] just to have a glimpse of their heroes' boots and even asking to touch them, as if drawing inspiration from some magical power."

And finally, as the bus was about to turn into London Road, it had just passed Celtic's first ground, located at the junction of Springfield Road and Janefield Street, and where a centre forward borrowed from Dumbarton, Johnny Madden, had played in the fledgling team's first-ever match, a 5-2 victory over a Rangers side in May 1888. The champions-elect of Europe had recently been re-acquainted with his missionary work on their Continental travels, more specifically Prague. Memories, memories…

All along the route it was as if every Celtic fan in the city was still in dreamland, still digesting and savouring the giddy realisation that their team, which had achieved local, then national fame, had just been catapulted into another, international dimension by 90 minutes of footballing brilliance watched by millions of television viewers. 24 hours earlier they had been gripped by tension. On the tenth anniversary of that triumph, Elizabeth Higgins of Reidvale Street (a mile from Celtic Park), told the *Celtic View* of "a night that will be with me always." Both she and her daughter had been allowed home an hour early from work to watch the match on television, and she recalled that at kick-off time "there wasn't a living soul in our street and where I lived there were about 100 children." Gripped by nerves when the time came to switch on the set, she grabbed a bucket and chamois and went into her bedroom "to clean the windows which had been washed two days earlier…" She noticed again how empty the street still was. However, in the closing stages of the final, "suddenly, in the house across the road, everyone was jumping around and shouting", prompting her to return to her living room, where her daughter stopped dancing around the room and threw her arms around her mother. "That was the end of the window cleaning. I grabbed my coat and ran and ran. As I got out, people were coming from their houses shouting 'We've done it! We've done it!'"

In similar vein, another fan remembered how the streets of Springburn, deserted during the game, suddenly came alive after the final whistle with jubilant singing Celtic fans decked in club colours celebrating in a manner akin to "one hundred New Years rolled into one", and there were newspapers reports of fans marching through the Celtic stronghold of the Gorbals singing, dancing and waving flags. Later that evening, thousands of Celtic fans would gobble up the first editions of the *Daily Record* and the *Scottish Daily Express* which became available from street vendors and at city-centre railway stations. Ten-year-old Jamie Fox, then a self-confessed "wee rascal" from Haghill, came to grief as a result of this mania. As he recalled to co-author Pat Woods in a recent interview, in the hope of curing his troublemaking antics he had been sent to his grandmother's tenement flat in Tureen Street (off the Gallowgate) for 'tobering', Glaswegian slang for 'sorting out'. He watched the final on a small television set in the company of his grandmother ('Granny' O'Hagan, a hawker who sold her goods, mainly clothing, in the nearby 'Barras' market) and her little wire-haired terrier Bimbo. A few hours after the match finished, he was sent out, as usual, to buy copies of the aforementioned newspapers at the corner of Bellgrove Street and the Gallowgate, but, as he passed by windows out of which flags and scarves were hung out in tribute to Celtic, he got caught up in the celebrations as the pubs came out. He joined in the singing and dancing, but became so wrapped up in the excitement of it all that he forgot all about his mission, and he was given a rude awakening when his granny suddenly appeared on the scene. She pulled him by the hair out of the crowds, gave him a clip on the ear and booted him up the backside, a 'skelping' of a type which was not unfamiliar in the West of Scotland in those un-PC days.

In contrast, regular customers of Doherty's pub in the Cowcaddens were able to toast Celtic's victory in champagne, courtesy of Scottish Television, whose own live *Scotsport* coverage of the final has been confined to obscurity - or even lost - given that the BBC footage has become so familiar. One wonders why, given the all-Scottish presentation by Alex Cameron (commentator), Bob Crampsey (studio link-man), and Arthur Montford, who was, apparently, in Doherty's to interview a set of noisy, boisterous customers alongside Bill Tennant, the presenter of the nightly *Here & Now* programme which followed immediately after the transmission of the match and who filled up the glasses of the celebrating customers with champagne. Sadly, the footage of this programme is also apparently missing.

On 'Welcome home night', May 26th, all roads led to Celtic Park. As the *Glasgow Herald* of May 27th 1967 put it: "This was an occasion for rejoicing. This team that had pulled itself up by its football boot straps out of the underprivileged East End of Glasgow had shown Europe how to play football and had broken the Latin grip on the European Cup." The trophy would be coming to a rather scruffy stadium in the poorest part of Glasgow, indeed one of the most disadvantaged spots in Europe, in sharp contrast to the homes of previous winners such as Real Madrid, Benfica and the Milan clubs. Hundreds of fans thronged the forecourt of Celtic Park hours before the Celtic bus was due to arrive. Many, including a large number of children, had climbed up the grassy slope to a disused railway line adjoining the ground or clambered onto the parapet of the bridge over the line in order to get a grandstand view of their heroes' arrival. "Green was everywhere, green bonnets, green scarves, green flags", said the *Scottish Daily Mail*, which also reported that, once the entrance doors to the stadium were opened, a fan scaled one of the 160-foot tall floodlight towers and balanced precariously on one of the girders.

Once again, Jamie Fox found the whole occasion getting the better of him. Sent out around teatime to get a copy of the *Evening Times*, he was making his way to a local newsagent when he noticed crowds congregating in the Gallowgate in the expectation of the Celtic bus passing that way en route to Parkhead. Suddenly, as the bus approached, Bobby Lennox and Jimmy Johnstone waved to him, or so it appeared to Jamie, who waved back, before running alongside a vehicle which was making slow progress along the Gallowgate. As he neared Celtic Park, he decided to take a short cut via Holywell Street, heading for the Janefield Street doors specially opened for the occasion and, once inside, he was given a punt up on top of one of the sheds belonging to R.D. Stewart, a local building contractors firm based in Wellshot Road, Shettleston, which was carrying out maintenance work in the stadium at the time; this proved to be an excellent vantage point for youngsters, one from which Jamie felt as if you could reach out and touch the players as the lorry circled the track. Alas, once again he had failed in his mission, and this time his granny administered a clip on the ear and he was sent to bed. However, as Jamie says, "it was all worth it."

Sheer hysteria reigned when the Celtic bus turned right on London Road into Kerrydale Street (a cul-de-sac recently absorbed into 'The Celtic Way' forecourt to the stadium) and nosed its way the few hundred yards up to the ground they call 'Paradise'. Jock Stein was not a man to openly display his emotions, according to his assistant Sean Fallon, but the latter said that, on this occasion, he dropped his guard: "When Jock Stein finally got off the bus at the main door, the flood gates opened and the tears started to fall from his eyes as he carried the Cup into the ground" (interview by Sam McLeod for the *Daily Mirror* of March 20th 2003 as part of the preview of the Liverpool vs. Celtic UEFA Cup match). Once inside, according to Jim Craig, the manager headed straight to the boot room to give "the first feel of the trophy" to the unsung old trainer-cum-scout Jimmy Gribben, who had been responsible for Jock Stein coming to Parkhead as a player and had encouraged the young and insecure provisional signing Jimmy Johnstone not to give up at a time when his future at the club was uncertain, to say the least. No Jimmy Gribben, you might say, no European Cup and the most glorious era in the Celtic story. Here was an unsung backroom employee of whom Stein once said: "No-one knew more about football than Jimmy Gribben. He taught me much, especially in my apprenticeship days as a coach and manager." A remarkable tribute, indeed.

"At Celtic Park", reported Hugh Cochrane, "everyone stamped enthusiastically to the sound of *The Holy Ground,* sung by The Clancy Brothers Irish folk group "as it thundered from the grandstand's loudspeakers", but it was a mere murmur compared to the moment when the victorious Celtic squad emerged from the tunnel: a screaming, cheering and chanting crowd estimated at between 50,000 to 70,000 fans went delirious with joy, the terraces erupting in a blaze of green and white banners. The use of a lorry, decked in the club's colours, as a means of parading the trophy and its winners, was entirely practical and wholly in keeping with an unpretentious organisation, and it enabled the circling of the stadium in such a manner as to give everyone present a good view of the proceedings. The lorry was not, in fact, a coal lorry (as is often stated), but one being used by contractors conducting important work for the club at the time. Any who may have thought this an unusual means of motorised celebration should note that seven years earlier, the Eintracht Frankfurt team had been paraded through the streets of their home city in a lorry belonging to a local brewery (Henninger's) - and they had lost the European Cup Final, in Glasgow, to Real Madrid, by a 3-7 margin!

A young schoolgirl would thus be afforded the privilege of a unique front seat view of the kaleidoscope of colour, noise and emotion that was Celtic Park on the evening that Scotland's finest brought the European Cup to the East End of Glasgow. Five-year-old Patricia McAlindon, the daughter of John, a former Celtic player turned the club's maintenance man and one of those popular, dedicated (indeed, indispensable) figures on whom football depends, had impressed on young Patricia that she would be a witness to a historic event as he lifted her into the cab of the R.D. Stewart lorry for its tour of the stadium. At her age, she may have found it difficult to take it all in, but what a memory! Preceded by the Coatbridge Shamrock Accordion Band playing supporters' favourites such as *The Celtic Song, Celtic, Celtic, That's the Team for Me* and *We Shall Not be Moved*, the lorry completed three laps of the track - briefly interrupted by a pitch invasion by excited youngsters - during which, according to *The Sun*, the mother of Bertie Auld shouted out "That's my boy!" as the lorry passed her, prompting supporters beside her to give her a hug. The event was marked by the sight of grown men with tears running down their cheeks. Celtic Park was a veritable kaleidoscope of joy before the proceedings drew to a close and the crowd reluctantly began to stream homewards, as if hoping there would be no end to an evening of sheer happiness, a moment in time when the *Daily Record* reporter seated in a plane hovering 3,500 feet above the stadium concluded that "It looked as if the whole city was pivoting around Celtic."

Fittingly, it would be left to James Gordon, the producer of the documentary titled *Celtic* from whose closing soundtrack the title of this chapter is taken, to grasp the significance of 'Lisbon' and its attendant celebrations for a (largely Catholic) community which had hitherto felt itself to be the underdogs in Scottish society: "One had a real sense that a victory on a football field had had a dramatic impact. For Celtic supporters, life would never be the same again, they had finally arrived." In September 1888, the fledgling club's first President, John Glass - a man committed to proving that "Irishmen could build a club as good as anyone" - had commented as follows on the hostile reception which the Celtic team had met ("abused on all sides" of the Exhibition Grounds, recalled ex-player Willie Maley) during their defeat by Cowlairs in the Glasgow Exhibition Cup final: "Let them scoff and jeer. Celtic will yet win to their proper position by their merits and those who scoff today will one day have to applaud." And now the hurrahs were ringing round a continent.

CHAPTER 14
'The Lisbon Lions'?

Lisbon 1967 has come to define Celtic FC, as defender Jim Craig mused in a fortieth anniversary interview with Phil Gordon published in the Scottish edition of *The Times*: "The 'Lisbon Lions' has become a well-known expression in Scottish life. We were lucky to play in the right place. If we had won in Paris, what would they have called us?" Yet how many are aware that the coining of the nickname, the only one of its type assigned to a European Cup/Champions League winning side (to the best of our knowledge), might not have become a reality? But for football politics and the issue of television coverage, the 1967 final would not have been played in the Portuguese capital at all!

May 25th 1967 in the *Estádio Nacional* was the culmination of a two-year saga marked by complacency (or, at best, misunderstandings) and deficiencies in communication, a story which had its origins in the bizarre and mysterious decision by UEFA in March 1965 to award that year's final to Milan instead of Rome, the expected choice. In recent times, the competition (renamed the Champions League in 1992) has now become so glamorous and surrounded by razzamatazz, so heavily underwritten by corporatism that, with the final being a guaranteed sell-out (with sponsorship restricting the availability of tickets to the 'ordinary' fans) due to the almost inevitable presence of at least one 'super club', that the venues can - and indeed, for commercial reasons, must - be announced two years in advance (for example, the choice of Cardiff for 2017 being announced in June 2015). In the early years of the competition, however, the drawing power of the potential finalists was a major, indeed crucial, consideration in determining the venue of the European Cup final, given that UEFA's only sources of revenue were the gate and television money. Thus the importance of the (enforced) belated decision-making in regard to that choice in order to maximise revenue: would, say, a Partizan Belgrade vs. Malmö encounter, with all due respect to both clubs, have 'bombed' at Real Madrid's Bernabeu Stadium?

UEFA's quandary in those days was obvious.

Italy, having supplied the previous two winners, in addition to two finalists and a semi-finalist, was a worthy recipient of the 1965 award, a first for the country. Benfica, twice winners in the early sixties, who had been defeated in the 1963 final at Wembley by one of the of Milanese giants, AC Milan, were certainly disadvantaged by the 1965 climax to the competition being played at the San Siro, home of holders Inter, a notoriously effective team which was managed with shrewd tenacity by Helenio Herrera, and which might have defeated the Portuguese at a genuinely neutral venue anyway. But Benfica were certainly unfortunate to some degree: not only did they have to cope with the pressure of playing a one-off fixture on their opponents' home pitch in heavy rain, which rendered the match virtually unplayable, but they also lost their goalkeeper to injury during the match (no substitutes were allowed then), and questions were asked about the refereeing of what was reportedly a very physical final. Benfica, who threatened to send a youth team or to boycott the match, were not alone in their protesting in vain about the apparent favouritism displayed in the choice of venue, with - for example - Robert Vergne of *L'Equipe*, after watching the "intimidating mass hysteria" (including the home fans' use of fireworks and smoke bombs) which had characterised Inter's ousting of Liverpool in the semi-finals, expressing his fear that the decision "endangered the very future of the tournament itself." The Portuguese football federation (FPF for short), furious that the decision had prevented their country's champions "from being able to face up to its opponent on equal terms", had even petitioned UEFA to have a replay, if needed, switched to Lisbon, a request which if successful would probably, in terms of rotation, have ruled out the 1967 final being played in their capital city even before what followed in 1966. Inter shrugged off the outcry surrounding the affair, but they felt the backlash two years later when they arrived in Lisbon to play Celtic, with Herrera forced on to the defensive when he insisted to a highly sceptical press that his club had had no part in the 1965 debacle ("entirely the fault of UEFA") while the club president Angelo Moratti tried to counter the residual ill-feeling by handing out complimentary match tickets, badges, etc. to the locals, a public relations gesture which may also have been one of making an apparent virtue out of his club's failure to sell out its ticket allocation. An unnamed FPF official took obvious pleasure in telling Marcel Clairen, who was covering the 1967 final for the Belgian newspaper *De Gazet van Antwerpen* that the Portuguese would be supporting Celtic because of the way Benfica had been treated. "Inter", he added, "need to be taught a lesson in humility."

To say that the Portuguese were suspicious of UEFA after these events, therefore, was an understatement. And, if the reasoning behind the selection of the venue for the 1965 final was obscure, then there was to be a further twist to the tale in 1966. In the quarter-finals, played in March that year, there was one outstanding tie: Manchester United vs. Benfica. With Inter and Real Madrid also still in the tournament, a glamour final seemed guaranteed, and Lisbon was clearly lined up as the venue for the final. The first spoke in the wheel of the bandwagon was inserted, unexpectedly, by the dazzling performance which sky-rocketed the precocious George Best to instant world fame. Manchester United had travelled to the *Estádio da Luz* anxiously for the return leg after eking out a 3-2 victory at Old Trafford. Benfica, undefeated at home in their previous nineteen ties in the competition and possessed of formidable attacking power, were clear favourites to progress to the semi-finals. However, two goals by the irrepressible Irishman in the first twelve minutes torpedoed the hopes of the home side, who exited the competition on an astonishing 3-8 aggregate which astounded the whole of Europe. For once the great Eusébio was overshadowed, evoking from him an assertion that "nothing can stop Manchester winning the European Cup."

Three days after that sensational triumph, the Portuguese *Record*, of March 12th 1966, quoted Matt Busby as very pointedly saying that he wanted to return to Lisbon for the final, a statement which followed one four days earlier by Helenio Herrera in *France Football* after his club had ousted Ferencváros: "If we have to meet Benfica, I would prefer to meet them in the semi-finals on a home and away basis, rather than in the final in Lisbon." Thus, the general consensus around Europe was that the Portuguese capital was the venue for the final. In its edition of March 17th 1966, *A Bola* (which appears to have been able to obtain stories from the FPF more readily than other Portuguese titles) took consolation for the nation's loss of face at the hands of the 'Red Devils' by stating, confessing even, that a fix had been engineered to right a wrong: "The bitter pill of the elimination of Benfica, the Portuguese representatives, has denied the country the reparation for the injustice which was done to it last season, when the final was assigned to the home stadium of one of the finalists. The UEFA decision to award the final to Lisbon before knowing the identity of the finalists may have been as unjust as last season's decision, but it shows some good conscience on the part of those in charge of European football that they did not hesitate to commit a new injustice in order to make up for the one of the previous year."

Two days later, however, on March 19th, the front page of *A Bola* led with the shocking news for its readers that even this crumb of comfort for Portuguese football fans was to be taken away from them, with the announcement that, as a result of deliberations at UEFA's meeting at Cannes the previous day, the 1966 final would now be held in Brussels. That same day, the 'Special Correspondent' of the *Glasgow Herald* gave a clear indication that a change of mind had taken place at UEFA, stating that the aforesaid meeting had "decided that the European Cup final (in which Manchester United may be concerned) will take place in Brussels and not Lisbon on May 11." The Spanish sports daily *Marca*, which on the morning of the meeting had stated categorically that the final would be in Lisbon, carried a headline the next day ('UEFA changes its mind, the European Cup final destined for Brussels') together with an observation: "From one day to the next, according to the Alfil news agency, UEFA has changed its mind. And where it previously said Lisbon, now it says Brussels." Quite apart from the apparent injustice to Portugal itself, eyebrows were raised in Lisbon at the decision to take the final back to a previous venue for the first time (the Heysel stadium had also been used in 1958) rather than taking the final for the first time to what was now well established as one of the great football cities on the continent. The Portuguese sporting press attempted to make sense of what seemed an outrageous *volte face*. No clear explanation ever emerged from UEFA regarding this decision in the Portuguese press, but, once again, the final would go ahead at a venue which was not well received in Portugal.

There was obviously some speculation as to the reasons for this decision. The most detailed reports on the issue available in Portugal (which are the most important ones in our context, since the questions raised potentially had some influence over the course of events when the final was played in Lisbon in 1967) were covered in *A Bola*. On March 19th, it sharply refuted suggestions emanating from *Gazzetta dello Sport* in Italy that the FPF had itself requested that it no longer wished to be considered as a host for the final, possibly as a consequence of Benfica's unexpected elimination. In its March 26th edition, *Record* carried the relevant extract from an FPF meeting of February 26th in regard to the staging of the match: "to accept definitively the proposal/offer from UEFA to organise the final of the European Champions' Cup in 1966." Four days later *A Bola* reproduced the text of a telegram sent on 28th February by the Portuguese authorities to UEFA, confirming that they would host the final, regardless of Benfica's participation or not: "Re your letter of 19th January, we propose organising the final of the European Champions' Cup in Lisbon. As well as any second game required within 48 hours. The stadium will be confirmed in due course depending on the progress of our representatives Sport Lisboa e Benfica." A follow-up letter to this telegram then claimed that both Benfica's own stadium and Sporting's Alvalade possessed excellent facilities for such a match (and it is interesting to note here, of course, that the National Stadium was not even considered as a possible candidate at that time), and Justino Pinheiro Machado, the President of the FPF, reassured the newspaper that the final would have produced around 4,000,000 *escudos* income (around £50,000 at the exchange rate current at the time), which he clearly regarded as a more than acceptable return for such a match. It was, in fact, roughly the sum raised by the 1967 final. Yet, as we shall see, there were some grounds for doubting the Federation's preparedness for hosting the 1966 final.

The decisive factor in the move away from Portugal appears to lie in the area of telecommunications: Portugal's state broadcaster, *Radiotelevisão Portuguesa* (RTP), had only just joined the Eurovision network on January 1st 1966, so that doubts existed about the important issue of television coverage of the match. *A Bola* on March 19th 1966 had quoted a Belgian journalist, Marcel de Leener, as indicating that there were serious doubts raised at the UEFA meeting in Cannes not only about the size of receipts from the final and the potential size of the crowd, but also about TV coverage, which become an issue after a British representative on Eurovision had, reportedly, said that Lisbon could not guarantee the twenty "foreign broadcast streams" required for the event. Matos Correia of RTP expressed his surprise to *A Bola* that Eurovision should think that Portugal "wasn't up to it", asserting that his organisation had been working actively on its preparations for the event. Justino Pinheiro Machado followed RTP in denying the accuracy of these assertions, and *A Bola* (not for the first time) was to make negative insinuations about the neutrality in this matter of Joseph Crahay, the Belgian president of UEFA, even though he insisted that he had left the committee room when Brussels was proposed as an alternative venue. Nonetheless, in the build-up to the aforementioned Benfica vs. Manchester United match, which had aroused widespread attention across Europe and attracted numerous journalists from third countries to cover a match at the Luz in which the crowd overflowed on to the track, it had been noted with some surprise by Antonio Valencia in *Marca* of March 9th, the day of the match, that the host club had turned down the lucrative opportunity to broadcast the match live via Eurovision and Intervision (the Eastern Bloc network), apparently on the grounds of wishing to guarantee a sell-out within the stadium. If this hinted at doubts surrounding the capacity of the state broadcaster RTP to transmit a match live to an international audience, then the lack of an explanation from RTP was clearly an opportunity lost to refute such reservations. The importance of TV coverage to UEFA, particularly as a source of revenue long before sponsorship came into play, was underlined by *Marca* reporting on March 18th 1966 the hesitation in confirming Hampden Park as the venue for the upcoming European Cup-Winners' Cup final (in which Celtic might well have been one of the participating finalists), the rider being that the match would be moved to Lausanne instead if the SFA could not satisfy them as to local capacity to 'stream' abroad a final in which Borussia Dortmund would beat Liverpool, Celtic's semi-final conquerors, in the latter's home city.

Significantly, there was both a degree of complacency at best and a serious lack of clarity on the part of the Portuguese regarding their attitude towards the event. On March 22nd 1966, *Record* (which generally was a little less respectful of the FPF than *A Bola*) reported that, on the day of the fateful executive meeting in Cannes, both Pinheiro Machado and his assistant, Afonso Lacerda, were, unaccountably, in Angola to deal with other business. The absence of the two senior representatives of the FPF at the meeting where the venue of the final was to be confirmed not only meant that there was nobody present to represent the country's interests when questions were raised about its suitability, but in addition it appears that the senior management of the FPF had been effectively thwarted in their ambitions by at least one of their own colleagues. UEFA's Vice-President, Agustín Pujol, was quoted in the Spanish sports newspaper *Marca* of March 24th 1966 as saying that "the Secretary of the Portuguese Football Federation had informed this [i.e. UEFA's] management group that, if Benfica was not taking part in the final, the interest which it had raised in Portugal was very much reduced." In his official statement, reproduced in the newspaper, Pujol added the following: "Important technical difficulties had emerged regarding the transmission of the match by television. Whatever, since Brussels was the second choice amongst the range of cities suitable for hosting the European Cup final and offered all kinds of guarantees in relation to technical [TV] expertise and financial success, the award of the final [to Brussels] was made in absolute unanimity." Max Urbini, writing in *France Football* of March 22nd, had already stated that the Belgian capital had been preferred to Lisbon ("which deserved the final ten times over") because - although he did not articulate his assertion at length - the Portuguese federation, presumably, could not increase the admission prices due to a government decree ["*ordonnance gouvernementale*"], while Brussels could double theirs and bring more money to UEFA's coffers (his allusion was to a sort of 'bread and circuses' policy designed by the Portuguese government to ensure that attendance at approved public events was feasible for a population which was relatively low-income in European terms). His verdict was backed on the day of the Real Madrid vs. Partizan Belgrade final, May 11th 1966, by a front page *L'Equipe* editorial which excoriated UEFA for seeing fit "to reject the legitimate and already approved candidature of Lisbon in favour of Brussels for clearly financial reasons, namely that the gate at the Heysel Stadium will be higher than the Portuguese capital could have delivered and, above all, higher television revenue will be achieved."

Pinheiro Machado's indignation at the decision (and his Secretary's apparent role in it) was not slow in forthcoming, but it was almost certainly no more than a case of locking the stable door after the horse had bolted: an interview with him (while still in Luanda), published in *Marca* on March 25th 1966, reveals some displeasure on the President's part with the Federation's (unnamed) Secretary, a man he said that he thought he had trusted and to whom he said that he was sending a personal telegram, in addition to the one which he would be sending to UEFA in the hope that the decision to stage the match in Brussels would be overturned. His feelings about his colleague were made clear by a sharp rebuke (never reproduced, to the best of our knowledge, in any Portuguese paper): "Where there is a President, a Secretary does not give the orders." It appears, therefore, that *Gazzetta dello Sport* had been correct: it had been the FPF's own Secretary who had hinted that the country might no longer wish to host the final, and the President's expressions of disapproval (fully a week after the decision had been taken) were, quite simply, far too little and far too late to have any influence over the allocation of the match. Pinheiro Machado was left to vent his frustration over the setback, and simultaneously put a brave face on the debacle, in his annual report published in the FPF yearbook covering season 1965-66: "It should be recorded with all due emphasis that Portugal has been entrusted with the organisation of the next [1967] final of the European Champions' Cup - to some degree, for sure, by way of compensation for the manoeuvres which prejudiced our federation last season. However, It does still, in any case, constitute a distinction which is worthy of note." No question about it, Portugal felt it had been treated shoddily (humiliated even), that UEFA's bolt from the blue was a slight on a small, poor country on the western fringes of Europe and one which would not have been considered in the case of larger football powers such as Spain or Italy.

It is thus no surprise after this row that there was an internal reorganisation of the management of the FPF in the summer of 1966 and that, in the FPF review of 1966-67, written after the Lisbon final, Justino Pinheiro Machado was to reflect in cryptic terms on how the FPF had, "in spite of all the prevailing circumstances, succeeded in carrying out the wishes of the previous management, by organising – with the success that Europe is familiar with – the final of the European Champions' Cup." In Portugal, a culture of respect for authority meant that it would have come as a surprise that internal feuds within national organisations should have been so readily exposed to public view, but the inference was clear: the FPF, under Pinheiro Machado's guidance, had pulled off a triumph in staging a final which (thankfully for him) had proved to be an undoubted success in terms of spectacle, regardless of any logistical difficulties glossed over by his claims. Regarding the 1966 final, however, *Record* had asserted that "previous practice more or less guaranteed that the final should be in Lisbon." Whatever, the further information gleaned from the reports in *Marca* in particular can only lead to the conclusion that UEFA could not safely go ahead with plans to award the match to Lisbon in that year. With all due sympathy to Portugal, despite its impressive contribution to European football in the first half of the 1960s, Brussels was a venue which had already been used successfully for the biggest event in European football, so that under the circumstances the change seems an entirely reasonable one, even if, with the benefit of hindsight, we must also remember the tragic events which were to tarnish the fourth final held there, the infamous one of 1985.

Nonetheless the vehemence of subsequent protests from Lisbon and Europe-wide press coverage sympathising with the Iberians clearly convinced UEFA that some reparation for two successive years of perceived slights to Portuguese football was essential. There was clearly also some degree of embarrassment within UEFA at the decision to replace Lisbon with Brussels, since at the meeting in Cannes it was decided that future venues would be decided well in advance, with changes being made only in cases of *force majeure*. Thus, the awarding of the 1967 final to Lisbon was made in London, in early July 1966 at a meeting held before the start of the World Cup Finals, a decision which came fully eight months earlier in the annual cycle than had been the case for the 1966 European Cup final. (The impression that this announcement may have been made to appease the FPF as a matter of urgency is perhaps supported by the fact that the Scottish Football Association, perhaps hoping to cash in on Celtic's success, decided in July 1967 to apply to host the 1968 final at Hampden, with no indication of when the outcome of this process would become known: clearly the process for 1968 was not regarded as having the same degree of urgency as it had had for 1967.) Equally, there was further evidence of fence-mending with the Portuguese, with Justino Pinheiro Machado being appointed in the summer of 1966 to the Organising Committee for the European Champions' Cup and Afonso Lacerda being given a place on UEFA's committees for junior tournaments and for the Inter-Cities' Fairs Cup.

UEFA'S 'treachery' was recalled periodically in the build-up to the 1967 final, and even after it. The lingering sense of grievance, mixed with glowing and justifiable pride at hosting one of the most memorable matches in football history, was expressed in the aftermath of that match by *A Bola's* sniping in its edition of May 27th 1967: "UEFA, who took the final away from Lisbon in 1966, must have had to swallow its pride when entrusting the organisation of the final [to Lisbon]. The Portuguese federation deserves to be congratulated." This was perhaps a response to a tactless statement in the match programme by UEFA President Gustav Widerkehr which touched on a still raw nerve by hinting that the host nation was somewhat backward: "For a long time already UEFA had wished to express its appreciation [of Portugal's contribution to the competition] by entrusting the Portuguese F.A. with the organisation of the Final Tie. The lack of installations for television transmission by Eurovision somewhat delayed the realization of this idea."

So, 'The Lisbon Lions'? We can never say for certain what might have happened if things had turned out differently in both 1965 and 1966, particularly in respect of the implications for the nickname of that hallowed team. Mere speculation, thankfully, for the only thing which matters is that, to paraphrase a well-known supporters' ditty, "We only know that there was indeed a show, and the Glasgow Celtic, they were there!" Amen to that.

CHAPTER 15
"Obrigado, Celtic."

Within two weeks of Celtic's Lisbon triumph, 120,000 spectators crammed into the Bernabeu stadium to pay homage to Real Madrid's Alfredo di Stéfano, in a testimonial match for the outstanding player of the first decade of the European Cup, but instead they ended up cheering a diminutive redhead, the inimitable Jimmy Johnstone, whose performance so captivated those present that at one stage in the match the crowd startled the winger in the midst of one of his mazy runs by rising to its feet to applaud his trickery. It was only fitting that he should create the winning goal (1-0) in the 70th minute, leaving several defenders trailing in his wake before sending a pass into the path of Bobby Lennox, whose crisp finish left Junquera helpless on a night when the latter's counterpart, John Fallon, made a significant contribution to Celtic's victory with a superb exhibition of goalkeeping.

It was both a prestigious way to bring down the curtain on an unforgettable season and also an opportunity for Celtic supporters to extend their basking in the reflected glory of what Jacques Ferran, one of the founders of the European Cup, described in *L'Equipe,* as "a resounding final, a spectacle blessed with sporting and human endeavour [which] has bolstered supporters of the European Cup against its critics." Lots of things, he added, contributed to the splendour of the final, the annual showpiece of the European game: "The wonderful setting of the national stadium, the sunshine, the crowd and the wonderful hospitality of the kindly Portuguese people. And then there was the match itself, profoundly reassuring for the health of our sport, and those of us who recalled the role of our newspaper in the birth of the competition could only take satisfaction. Above all, a glowing tribute must be paid to Celtic. The Scottish club has reasserted the basic values of moral and physical fitness, of *esprit de corps,* of adventurousness and of the sheer pleasure in playing the game. They have injected a breath of fresh air into our game. Thanks to them, it seems that the European Cup has been given a new lease of life" (May27/28th 1967 weekend edition).

Ferran's verdict was to be a constant, Continent-wide refrain which has resonated down the years. Simultaneous with his contribution was J. Simon's eulogy for "a brilliant and masterful exhibition of football" in the Brussels newspaper *Le Peuple* below a headline which hailed "the extraordinary Scottish triumph in Lisbon which has captivated the Portuguese public and millions of television viewers across Europe, Glasgow Celtic have rendered football its greatest and most timely service", while Gameiro Pereira of the Portuguese *Record* welcomed the "Longed-for destruction of defensive football which has been so damaging to the sport." The correspondent of *L'Aurore* (Paris) reinforced the perception that Celtic's display had breathed vitality and positive thinking back into the game with his observation that the Glasgow club had "rehabilitated attacking football and its element of risk, the very essence of the sport", while Heinz Engler, chief football writer of the German news agency DPA, said that Celtic did "more than win the European Cup, they also gave an incredible demonstration of attacking football once written off as dead."

This sense that Celtic had rescued the very competition itself (even if only in terms of its image) was being expounded by members of the Continental press who were aware of the disillusionment that had set in with a tournament that had seemed to have run its course by the mid 1960s and was believed by some to be beyond redemption. An example of this was the coverage by the French magazine, *Miroir du Football*, of Inter Milan's 1965 semi-final second-leg win over Liverpool, headlined as a victory in the San Siro for chauvinism, and which depicted the European Cup as a competition which had lost its sheen and was "bent on suicide." The match report depicted a contest played in front of an 80,000 crowd which took hostility to an unprecedented level of hysteria. The main theme was the *réalisme* (French for a combination of pragmatism and cynicism) which had crept into the game. That perception was reinforced by the final itself, also played in the San Siro, where Inter were quite content to hold on to a 1-0 lead against a Benfica team down to ten men, with a defender (Germano) taking over in goal after goalkeeper Costa Pereira went off injured. It would be two years before substitutes were allowed in UEFA competitions. Meanwhile, Ferran's colleague and fellow co-founder (indeed the inspiration) of the European Cup, Gabriel Hanot, had been expressing his reservations about his brainchild, fearing that it was turning into some sort of 'Frankenstein's monster' and lamenting its decline due to the greed for money of the big clubs which he linked to the pernicious influence of a win-at-all-costs philosophy with its inevitable accompaniments of violent play, unacceptable crowd behaviour, suspect refereeing and defensive football. Little wonder then that as recently as June 2015 *France Football* should regard the 1967 version as one of the most significant and memorable European/Champions League finals when paying tribute to "the wonderful Lisbon Lions."

Indeed, Jock Stein himself, rarely a man to go overboard about his many triumphs, conveyed a sense that his team's performance in the 1967 final had acquired a significance which transcended the lifting of yet another trophy when he replied as follows to a reader's question posed to him in Norman Giller's weekly 1970s 'Sports Forum' in the *Daily Express*. "There was not a prouder man on God's earth than me the night we won the Cup in Lisbon. Winning was important, aye, but it was the way that we won that filled me with satisfaction. We did it by playing football. Pure, beautiful, inventive, positive football. There was not a negative thought in our heads. Inter played into our hands. It was sad to see such gifted players as they had shackled by a system that restricted their freedom to think and to act. Our fans would never accept that style of sterile approach. Our objective has always been to win with style" (quote reproduced in Giller's 2003 book *McFootball*).

That Celtic's feat went beyond the mere bringing of the Cup across the Channel (or just to northern Europe, for that matter) for the first time was also emphasized by James Lawton's statement in *The Independent* of May 22nd 2007 that there should be no question, "no loose talk", regarding the greatest achievement ever by a British club in Europe: "That is a place in history which, for all the achievements of Bob Paisley, Joe Fagan, Brian Clough, Sir Mark Busby and Sir Alex Ferguson, still belongs to Jock Stein. When the Celtic manager took his team to Lisbon to break down the bolted door of Helenio Herrera's Internazionale in 1967, he declared that his deepest ambition was a victory for football, something to thrill every neutral. He felt he owed that much to the game and he produced his extraordinary gift with 11 players bred in a 30 mile radius of Glasgow." That final sentence touches upon a phenomenon that never ceases to amaze and is unlikely ever to be paralleled, as Gabriele Marcotti suggested: "The more you think about it, the more improbable it seems. A city produces enough good players to make the starting 11 of the best team in Europe and they all play for the same club, at the same time" (*Champions* magazine, June/July 2007 edition).

The greatest satisfaction that Chairman Bob Kelly and Jock Stein took from that historic day was the knowledge that it was a trophy won largely (with a couple of exceptions) by players nurtured within the club. When asked once by BBC TV commentator, John Motson for his outstanding recollection of the occasion, Stein focused on his feelings just before kick-off: "Here was a group of players who had been attached to the club almost from boyhood. We were almost a home-grown team, but we were playing the might of European football. A club (Inter Milan) who bought players not only in Italy, but throughout the world. For the first time, we thought here was a foreign team afraid of a British team."

The boys of '67 were very much of their time, a grounded bunch who never lost touch with their roots. In 2003, Martin O'Donnell, a Celtic fan brought up in West Lothian where his father "worked all the overtime available to feed and clothe seven kids, not easy on a labourer's wage" and to whom the recently acquired television set on which the family and his workmates watched the 1967 final "seemed like a luxury in his eyes", recalled in the fanzine *More than 90 minutes* coming away from a recent visit to the *Estádio Nacional* emotionally drained after replaying the game in his head, "assailed with images, voices and colours and people from the past... and a way of life that has gone, never to return." Reflecting on the social and sporting changes of recent decades which he said had been driven by consumerism, he concluded that Lisbon should be seen for what it was, "a wonderful night in a wonderful place" at a marvellous period in the club's history, one made possible by "players who looked and sounded just like us, because they were just like us: they knew what it was to play for Celtic and represent their fans." Half a century on, the continuous feting by Celtic fans of the Lisbon Lions, a matter of astonishment to the squad itself, reflects a unique affinity. No other winners of the European Cup/Champions League have come remotely close to receiving the level of adulation and reverence that has been bestowed on Celtic's finest.

It is a phenomenon that is all the more remarkable given that the post-Bosman football landscape has virtually ensured that, for the foreseeable future at least, Celtic will never reach such giddy heights again. Romance, tradition and sentiment has been all but expunged from what was once called the people's game, as exemplified by *L'Equipe*'s Spanish correspondent Frédéric Hermel stating in September 2016, following a heavy defeat at the hands of Barcelona, that Celtic didn't even deserve to be in the Champions League. In similar vein, dazzled by the riches available from broadcasting rights, sponsorship and marketing opportunities, UEFA has become a virtual prisoner of Europe's wealthiest clubs, an organization bullied in late 2016 into endorsing a proposal to grant free passage (*risque zéro*, as *Le Monde* described it) to the group stages of the Champions League for the top four clubs from Spain, Germany, Italy and England, a move widely seen as a stepping stone to an elite, self-elected club Super League created by a possible breakaway from UEFA: in October 2016 the newly-elected UEFA president Aleksander Ceferin hinted that Champions League finals could soon be played in cities outside Europe, with New York being cited as an ideal candidate, in order to tap into the growing interest in the game in the United States. There is a sense of inevitability about the increasing drift to the 'monetisation' of the sport, a development underlined perhaps by the April 2016 Quarter-Final first leg match between *nouveau riche* clubs, Paris Saint-Germain and Manchester City, an artificial contest in every respect, one characterised by *The Times* as "The great petrodollar derby", a proxy Qatar vs. Abu Dhabi contest "built around Arab oil wealth, with European football serving as a vehicle for a global statement of ambition." The term "Franchise football" has been used to describe the closed-shop mentality that is seemingly driving football's elite, and it is an outlook that may well prevail as the wind of change blows through football. After all, who, back in 1967, could have envisioned the transformations wrought in regards to the identities of the finalists? Celtic, then a limited liability club under the dynastic control of the Kelly and White families, became a PLC after Fergus McCann's takeover in 1994, a transformation dwarfed in June 2016 when Inter Milan, for nearly six decades the fiefdom of the Moratti family, was taken over by Suning Holdings Group, a Chinese retail giant.

In an era of bewildering social, political and sporting change, it comes perhaps as a relief to dwell on simpler times, to indulge in a spot of reverie. In the mind's eye of those whose experience of the event has never left them, it is forever close to 5:30 on a sultry afternoon in a sun-dappled amphitheatre when suddenly, as if from nowhere, two teams wearing classically famous, vividly contrasting jerseys emerge from an underground tunnel to release the pent-up anticipation of a crowd whose explosion of noise and colour already indicates a partiality for the eleven men in green and white marching towards that moment of decision characterised by one writer as the "absolute edge of no return", but who were, in truth, striding towards immortality.

Simpson, Craig, Gemmell...